THE DYSLEXIC SCHOLAR

THE
DYSLEXIC
SCHOLAR
HELPING YOUR CHILD
SUCCEED IN THE SCHOOL SYSTEM

Kathleen Nosek

Taylor Publishing
Dallas, Texas

*To all my friends, clients, and colleagues,
and, especially, to my grandson, Chris.*

Published by Taylor Publishing Company
          1550 West Mockingbird Lane
          Dallas, Texas 75235

Library of Congress Cataloging-in-Publication Data

Nosek, Kathleen.
    The dyslexic scholar; helping your child succeed in the school system / Kathleen Nosek.
        p.   cm.
    Includes bibliographical references and index.
    ISBN 0-87833-882-9
    1. Dyslexic children—Education—United States. 2. Education—Parent participation—United States. I. Title.
    LC4709.N67 1995
    371.91'44—dc20   94-45423
                                                                    CIP

Printed in the United States of America

10 9 8 7 6 5 4 3 2 1

CONTENTS

INTRODUCTION

There are thousands of books, pamphlets, and teaching materials on the subject. In fact, there is more written about dyslexia than any other type of known learning disability. So why a how-to book on dyslexia? What's yet unsaid? Dyslexia is a little-understood, hidden complaint that's passed back and forth between educators, physicians, psychologists, and opportunists. Dyslexia has always been a political hot potato nobody wants to claim. Educators assert children "outgrow" dyslexia, so we are not to worry. To many physicians, dyslexia is a total mystery and an undramatic one at that. Psychologists experiment with behavior modification. Scam artists promise to deliver quick fixes. How confusing this is for the layperson, and how humiliating for the dyslexic child or adult.

In truth, dyslexics are "normal" individuals who mask their learning disability by compensating in other ways. Many are average; some are below average. Others, like Albert Einstein, Thomas Edison, and Winston Churchill, achieve prominence through extraordinary achievement.

After 10 years of fighting the public school system in Texas in an effort to secure services for my dyslexic grand-

1

son, I decided it was time to share my experience in helping dyslexic children and adults. Let me assure you there is hope, and a way to win the battle, even though it seems the odds are stacked against you.

After a twenty-year career, during which I taught school, tutored, worked as a mental-health counselor, lectured, presented seminars, provided in-service training for other teachers, and edited *The Language Link* (a news bulletin), I went to serve as executive director of National Dyslexia Referral Center (NDRC).

At NDRC, a nationwide provider of dyslexia-related information and referrals, it soon became evident that no matter how much help we provided, the chasm between delivery of crucial information and implementation of the data was a nightmare for most callers. Responding to the need for how-to information became NDRC's most pressing mission, and often, even then we were unable to meet the public's needs.

Despite all the legislative mandates, both federal and state, and despite all NDRC's efforts to educate the public, nothing has changed in our schools! Dyslexia is still a closeted disorder; schools would rather label children as behavior problems than diagnose dyslexia. The end result is the public schools' failure to educate, and a drop-out rate that is worse than ever.

I attribute the basic problem to these simple facts:
• Teacher training—poor or nonexistent
• Basic information—poor access for the layperson
• Shame—dyslexia is considered synonymous with "dummy."

In response, I offer a step-by-step guide through the labyrinth of what to do when. So before you spend big bucks, waste time, and endure unnecessary heartache, get the facts first.

Much of the published literature concerns research, remediation, "cures," psychological implications, and management techniques. For those who wish to pursue these aspects, I include an extensive bibliography.

Also, I use the "D" word, dyslexia, without apology. Let's call it what it is: dyslexia=trouble with words. Now, let's see how to make life more manageable for dyslexic children (and adults), including those dyslexic school administrators and teachers out there…you know who you are.

1 UNDERSTANDING DYSLEXIA

The term dyslexia comes from the Greek root "dys" (trouble) and "lexia" (word). Thus, dys^lexia means "trouble with words." What kind of trouble? Simply put, dyslexia means trouble with reading, writing, and spelling.

This trouble can be expressed in a number of ways, including some of these commonly heard complaints: "I spell perfectly—it's my handwriting that's so awful" or "I can read; I just can't remember what I've read" or "It takes me forever to figure out the words; I can't spell worth a darn, so I lose my concentration and give up."

Sound familiar? This happens to all of us at one time or another. Our previously beautiful handwriting becomes sloppy; we're distracted and lose our place while reading; we misspell words out of carelessness or just plain forgetfulness. Before you come unglued, take a deep breath.

What I just described is normal for most of us. We catch our error right away and correct it. However, for 25 million Americans, it is normal to experience all of the above *all of the time* and not know the difference.

Impossible, you say. How could this happen? These people must be lazy. If they paid attention in school, they wouldn't make such stupid mistakes. What's the big deal? If children choose to be lazy and inattentive at school, that's their problem. But what about children who do not choose to be lazy, who pay attention, give it their best shot, and still can't read?

THE DILEMMA

According to some educators, dyslexia is a figment of our imagination. Other proponents of the out-of-sight, out-of-mind theory say dyslexia is a medical problem and must be treated outside the school. Educators find it much easier to pin the blame for a child's reading difficulties on family problems, television, or the weather. To them, playing the blame game makes more sense than recognizing and taking responsibility for remediating dyslexia.

"But-t-t-t...," the educators sputter, dyslexia is a disease and needs to be treated by medical doctors.

Says who? Don't believe that assertion for one minute.

"But-t-t-t...," the educators sputter again, dyslexics are doomed; they can't go to college or get a job.

Aha! That's my favorite answer. Ever hear of Tom Cruise? Agatha Christie? Woodrow Wilson? Nolan Ryan? These individuals are classic examples of dyslexics who beat the odds and became successful.

Now you are really confused. Just exactly what is dyslexia?

Here's a sampling of viewpoints that are generally accepted as theoretically sound and describe the issue quite well.

- **Margaret B. Rawson, past president of the Orton Dyslexia Society** (in *Annals of Dyslexia*, 1985)— "Dyslexia is a condition manifested by difficulty with learning to read and write efficiently despite the presence of normal intelligence, adequate educational opportunities, and normal psychiatric make-up."
- **Texas Scottish Rite Hospital, Child Development Division**—"Specific dyslexia is a developmental language disability that involves difficulty with the symbols of written language. By definition, this disability includes basic problems in learning the alphabet and its phonic properties, in word recognition, reading, reading comprehension, copying and spelling."

• **Dr. Manuel Gomez, pediatric neurologist, Mayo Clinic**—"There are more dyslexic children needing recognition and special teaching than all of the deaf, blind, and retarded put together."
• **Drs. Silver and Hagin, Department of Neurology and Psychiatry, New York University, Bellevue Medical Center**—"If a child is seriously retarded in reading and has normal intelligence, chances are about 9 in 10 that he has a specific language disability (dyslexia)."
• **Frances K. McGlannon, Director of the McGlannon School**—"It would be difficult, if not impossible, to find any other disability affecting an estimated six million children in the United States today, on which so much research has been done, so many thousands of articles written, and yet concerning which so very little information has reached the average teacher or pediatrician, to say nothing of parents and public. These children are as handicapped by the ignorance surrounding their problems as they are by the problem itself."

HOW MANY PEOPLE ARE DYSLEXIC?

The statistics vary. The National Center for Educational Statistics reports 5 to 15 percent of school children are dyslexic. The U.S. Department of Health Education and Welfare sets the figure at 15 percent of the total population. OSERS, the Office of Special Education and Rehabilitative Services, reports 1 out of every 7 people in the U.S. is dyslexic. Professionals who work in the field say the actual figure is closer to 20 percent of the total population. For the sake of compromise, I will use a median figure of 10 percent. So, statistically, we can say there are approximately 25 million dyslexics in the United States.

WHO IS DYSLEXIC?

Here's the breakdown:
Sex: Predominantly male (70 to 80 percent).
Race: All ethnicities are affected.
Onset: Usually becomes evident during school years.
Family Pattern: Common among first-degree biological relatives.

Course: Lifelong disorder, depending on degree of severity.
Physical Symptoms: None. Hidden disability.

Dyslexia is more prevelant in males because boys are more readily identified through undesirable behavior. Classroom teachers focus on these kids immediately because they misbehave. Female dyslexics usually don't make waves and learn to hide their deficiency behind a shy or quiet personality. Teachers experiencing behavior problems in the classroom seldom suspect dyslexia or some other kind of learning problem, *even when the student is failing or performing below average.* Behavior becomes the focus and therein lies the predicament.

IS IT GENETIC OR BEHAVIORAL?

Dyslexia was first recognized as a learning disability in 1896 by two English physicians, Kerr and Morgan, who called it "word blindness." This launched the confusing and erratic history of at least 35 definitions for the disorder and a lengthy list of descriptive diagnoses recorded in the literature.

In 1925, Dr. Samuel Torrey Orton announced a plan to conduct research in cerebral physiology for his clients who exhibited "a very special disturbance of the ability to learn to read." However, lack of funding prevented the fulfillment of his ambition until half a century later. Then, Dr. Albert M. Galaburda made an astonishing discovery that validated Orton's original theory: the localized section of the brain that directs all aspects of reading skill is different in dyslexics. The anomaly or altered development exists in the formation of the cortex on the left side of the brain and is considered an significant cause of dyslexia.

More recently, a research group at Rutgers University reported that the fundamental problem of dyslexic children lay with the fast processing cells in the auditory cortex of the brain. The findings reported in August 1994, by Dr. Paula Tallal and other researchers, suggested that dyslexia is, at root, a flaw in a specific brain circuit that handles rapidly flowing information. The research of Galaburda and Tallal point to the fast processing cells, both visual and auditory, as culprits in the learning problems of dyslexic children. The big task for researchers has been to pinpoint the cause of the malfunction and determine whether it is connected with a genetic cell deficiency, and/or if it involves larger brain circuits and occurs during brain development. Then, in the fall of 1994, a major discovery that supports the gene basis theory was announced by another research team.

In October 1994, I talked with Dr. William Kimberling and Dr. Shelly Smith at Boys Town National Research Hospital in Omaha about their exciting genome research. Drs. Kimberling and Smith are part of a research team that traced a genetic basis for dyslexia to a small region of chromosome 6. The evidence was duplicated after years of study involving extended families and a group of twins. Research teams tracked genetic material taken from 358 members of 19 families, about 60 percent of whom had dyslexia. Studies of 50 pairs of twins and their families yielded even more conclusive evidence. The study results affirm speculation, from Dr. Orton's time to the present, that dyslexia has a genetic component. But don't be alarmed. This is good news for dyslexics! Now that dyslexia can be considered a real biological disorder, early screening (in infants at birth) may become routine, ultimately leading to a reliable, universally accepted diagnosis and earlier, more effective treatment.

For the purpose of this book, we shall use the behavioral viewpoint rather than focus on the scientific nature of dyslexia. The behavioral approach includes a genetic component, with the observation that dyslexia tends to run in families. Until scientific research or genetic engineering proves otherwise, we shall concentrate on immediate, proven, and practical measures.

THE CURES

The old piece of advice "Buyer beware" still rings true, even for the most tantalizing "cure" for dyslexia. I strongly urge you to heed such advice when investigating the various resources available. I do not pass judgment on the methods outlined below. Each has its champions.

However, before you spend one penny, carefully research each method's documented long-term results. Then make an educated decision, based on your common sense and willingness to pay.

1. Vision therapy—Visual motor coordination and integration (eye exercise) develops visual-physical skills so the patient can function as a coordinated whole. Dr. Leonard White is a pioneer in this field and says "the basic problem is coordination and integration of the neurological patterns that create...adequate responses of the body as a whole." Although Orton's original observation that visual perception is normal for the majority of dyslexics still holds true, even today there is considerable debate among ophthalmologists regarding the validity of eye exercise for dyslexics. The American Federation of Ophthalmologists released this statement in 1981 concerning eye exercise and dyslexia: "No known scientific evidence supports claims for improving the academic abilities of dyslexic...children...with treatment based on visual training, including muscle exercises, ocular pursuit or tracking exercises, or glasses..."

2. Inner ear imbalance—Dr. Harold Levinson discovered an ear-dyslexia connection when his research indicated that dyslexics suffered from balance and coordination problems as well as motion sickness. When clients were treated with motion-sickness medicine, their reading problems eased. However, Dr. Levinson says special education, occupational therapy, eye-tracking exercises, and physical exercise are also useful.

3. Kinesiology—Educational kinesiology is a system of brain-integration exercises designed to help learning-disabled children achieve static balance skills. Improvement in academic performance has been demonstrated, but studies to date for a specific relationship to dyslexia remediation have not been conducted in a scientific manner. Results, although encouraging, are not quantifiable.

4. Colored glasses—The Irlen light-filtering glasses have been shown to improve the visual skills of some scotopic-sensitive dyslexics (those who are sensitive to specific wavelengths of light, causing perception problems). However, treating Scotopic Sensitivity Syndrome with spectrally modified lenses does not rule out other problems associated with dyslexia. For those suffering from visual distortions, which makes perception a hampering factor in reading, the glasses minimize the distortion process.

The list goes on and on. The basic point to remember is this: there's no such thing as a quick fix for dyslexia. Your job is to work on patience and understanding. The dyslexic child's job is to pace himself and fine-tune shortcuts. Together, patience and self-pacing work wonders.

KNOW THE FACTS

A policy statement from the American Academy of Pediatrics, the American Academy of Ophthalmology, and the American Association for Pediatric Ophthalmology and Strabismus (1984) supports the position that a child or adult with dyslexia or a related learning disability should receive:

1. Early medical, educational, and/or psychological evaluation and diagnosis.

2. Remediation with educational procedures of proven value, demonstrated by valid research.

A summary of the conclusions endorsed by the three professional groups include:

1. Learning disabilities, including the dyslexias...may require a multidisciplinary approach from medicine, education, and psychology in evaluation, diagnosis, and treatment.

2. Eye care should never be instituted in isolation when a person does have dyslexia....

3. The teaching of dyslexic and learning-disabled children is a problem for educational science.

4. [We]...strongly support the early diagnosis and appropriate treatment of persons with dyslexia and related learning disabilities.

A revised policy statement, issued by the group in March 1992, states: "Eye defects, subtle or severe, do not cause reversal of letters, words, or numbers. No scientific evidence supports claims that the academic abilities of dyslexic or learning disabled children can be improved with treatment based on (A) visual training, including muscle exercises, ocular pursuit, tracking exercises, or 'training' glasses (with or without bifocals or prisms); (B) neurological organizational training (laterality training, crawling, balance board, perceptual training); or (C) tinted or colored glasses".

Furthermore, the group expressed concern about "the false sense of security which may delay or prevent proper remediation" and that some individuals may attempt to substitute unwarranted expense outlay for appropriate remedial education measures.

The emphasis on remedial education is the key. Experts in every profession agree on one point: remediation is essential. It is the function of schools to academically prepare students for their tasks as adults. Further, it is the responsibility of schools to teach children the way they learn.

To remediate is to help children learn by using a different method of teaching. The dyslexic cannot decode words; the majority of classroom children learn this process well enough. The dyslexic falls further and further behind; the majority of students progress, even with variations in teaching quality. Ordinary instruction fails to produce results and will continue to fail. No amount of reteaching works. It is the *method* that makes the difference. The knowledge that dyslexics are educable and, above all, want to learn is inspiration enough to warrant extra effort in the form of teacher-training programs.

Finally, not to complicate the matter, but rather to clarify, these are learning disorders that can accompany dylexia or appear separately:

Dysnomia—trouble with naming objects
Dyscalculia—trouble with arithmetic or math
Dysgraphia—trouble with writing

DYSLEXIA LOOKS LIKE THIS

The following letter is a classic example of a dyslectic college student, who in this case is writing to her advisor:

Dear Dr. Miller,

I am writting due to my sever problem of Dyslexia in mathmatics, spesificly college algebra. I have taken high school algebra three times, adn failed it twice. I've rigistered collge algebra four times dropped it three times and failed it once. My test scores passed on along by the Texas Rehabilitation Center verify that I have a problem with math. If there is any possiblity way you could wavie the class requierment for my degree plan or replace it with some other course more petainent to my major I would greatly appreciate it. My major is Family Studies and do not feel algebra to be as nessary as it would be for other majors. Thank-you for your consideration in this matter.

Sincerely,

Karen Smith

Briefly, let me tell you about Karen. She is tall, beautiful, dark-haired, and severely dyslexic. To her credit, Karen learned how to use the system. The system I refer to encompasses myriad local, state, and federal assistance programs already in place, just waiting for you.

By the way, Karen is presently enrolled in a master's program and is employed as a case worker for abused children. Her problem with dyslexia hasn't changed, but she is plugging away, with the help of some wonderful teachers, no doubt. Karen's success story can be your child's success story.

A TESTIMONIAL

An interesting letter appeared in the *Wall Street Journal*, Friday, January 20, 1989. It was from a man familiar with all the classic tribulations of a dyslexic firsthand. The letter underscores two points. One is the pervasiveness of dyslexia in a society that requires literacy as a passport to acceptance. The other is a professional opinion expressed by the writer concerning vision and dyslexia:

...Since I have been a dyslexic person, I personally can relate to the problems of learning.

Back in the 1920s, when I was in the lower grades of school, I was considered lazy, dumb or more likely both. Getting through the University of Pennsylvania was not only a struggle but also filled with many frustrations. After graduation and working for several years, which had a very sobering influence, I took an aptitude test given by Stevens Institute in Hoboken, N.J. Since I was from a family of doctors and was expected to go to medical school, but not wanting to flunk, I put off this effort. However, Stevens pointed out my dyslexic problem, and told me how to overcome it by memorizing the professors' notes and reading abstract summaries, etc. Thus, I was enrolled in medical school and attended Jefferson in Philadelphia. I never had less than a "B" average. To this day, I still continue to read abstract summaries and browse the literature that is interesting and necessary for my profession.

Being an ophthalmologist, I see many children whose parents bring them in the hopes that their learning difficulties are due to their eyes. This is seldom the case, but an explanation to the parents helps them to understand and cope with the learning problems that dyslexia presents.

Davis G. Durham, M.D.

DYSLEXIA AND ILLITERACY

Illiteracy was a common fact of life several generations ago. Our ancestors lived in an agrarian society, in which survival depended on hard work and stamina. As our society has evolved, the written word has become the key to survival and the measure of a person's worth.

Illiteracy is now shameful. For millions of dyslexics who hide their shame, the ability to read, write, or spell seems beyond their reach. As a result, we have within our society countless young people who are caught in a cycle of hopelessness.

As a professional counselor, my interaction with dyslexic children and adults focuses primarily on reversing their loss of hope. Everyone needs something definite to hang on to. I emphasize that the special, unique value of each dyslexic person is irreplaceable.

Along these same lines, parents should be aware that one of the warning signs of suicidal behavior is severe depression due to school pressure or failure. I believe the opposite is actually true. The way I see it, a history of learning disabilities combined with a sense of failure *causes* the depression, creating a vicious cycle of decline in school performance and increased behavior problems. The solution is simple: intervene; identify; remediate. Who needs to take the first step? **You take the first step**.

Don't wait for someone else to do it for you. If you suspect your child might be dyslexic, grab the bull by the horns. If you are an adult and recognize dyslexia in yourself, don't suffer in silence; it's never too late. I'll lead the way and show you how to take that first step.

BOOKS OF INTEREST

Critchley, MacDonald. *The Dyslexic Child.* 2nd Ed. London: Redwood Press Unlimited, 1972.

Reviews the problem of dyslexia from a neurologist's viewpoint. Includes a summary of research and well-documented review of dyslexia.

Flesch, Rudolf. *Why Johnny Can't Read: And What You Can Do About It.* New York: Harper Collins, 1986.

Addresses the American system of teaching, which fails to teach children how to master the mechanics of reading. Contains material and instruction for teaching children at home using the traditional method of alphabetic phonics.

Hornsby, Beve, Ph. D. *Overcoming Dyslexia.* New York: Arco Publishing Co., 1984.

Describes dyslexia, provides case histories to help readers understand it, and charts a specific course of action.

Jordon, Dale R. *Overcoming Dyslexia In Children, Adolescents, and Adults.*

Describes the various forms of dyslexia and relates those patterns to the social, emotional, and personal development of dyslexic individuals. Order from: PRO-ED, 8700 Shoal Creek Boulevard, Austin, TX 78757-6997.

Orton, Samuel Torrey, M.D. *Reading, Writing, and Speech Problems In Children.* New York: W.W. NORTON & CO., 1937.

A classic edition of Orton's theories and associated educational practices. Includes selected papers of Orton's work. Order from: PRO-ED, 8700 Shoal Creek Boulevard, Austin, TX 78757-6997.

2 THE IDENTIFYING AND TESTING PROCESS

A re you ready to take a look at the identification of dyslexia? Parents and teachers alike find the following list of characteristics a helpful decision-making tool. Keep in mind, identification is perhaps the most crucial step you will ever take.

A PLACE TO START

A checklist can help you spot a child or adult who may be dyslexic. Remember the checklist is for *identification* purposes only. Because you have to start someplace, the checklist remains a good first step toward identifying the problem. When using the checklist, be aware that the characteristics do not always appear at once, but appear over a period of time. Also, an isolated indicator is not significant but five or more indicators *are* significant.

The question "What is dyslexia?" is often answered by "Isn't that when someone reads or writes backwards?" Reading backwards or mirror writing can occur with dyslexia, but usually does not. The following characteristics are more common.

DYSLEXIA CHECKLIST
Preschoolers

- Do not understand what others are saying to them.
  (You have to repeat the statement two or three times.)
- Are unable to follow directions.
  (Child can't follow simple commands or gets confused and does the opposite.)
- Have difficulty remembering words and expressing them.
  (Child can't recall names of objects or gets words mixed up; i.e. "mine" and "yours".)
- Are uncertain of preferred handedness.
  (Ambidexterity is not uncommon in a very young child; however, preferred handedness usually becomes evident when he writes, plays ball, or reaches for objects.)
- Cannot recall letters of alphabet and avoid listening to stories read to them.
  (Can sing the alphabet but cannot recite it; restless or bored while being read to.)
- Have poor small-motor control.
  (Can't hold pencil, can't tie shoe, and/or can't cut with scissors.)

School-Age Children

- Are highly verbal and interested, but have difficulty learning to read.
  (Appears bright and aware of activities, but reading ability is far behind classmates.)
- Have confusion with sequencing letters in spelling.
  (Writes "wavie" instead of "waive".)
- Continue to reverse (*d* for *b*), transpose (*tranpsose*), and invert (*q* for *p*) letters in words and numbers.
- Write illegibly and misform letters/numbers.
  (Scribbles rather than writing in concise print or cursive; letters different size; no distinction between upper- and lower-case letters.)
- Have unreliable sense of direction.
  (Get confused with left, right; up, down; front, back.)
- Fall below grade level in reading, spelling, and writing *or*

succeed with reading, but continue to misspell and write illegibly.
- Leave out short words when reading, or add words not there.
  (Often add or leave out a short word like "not," which totally changes the meaning of sentence.)
- Complain of words running off the edge of page.
  (Usually starts to happen after reading two or three paragraphs.)
- Demonstrates an academic achievement level that does not match intelligence.
  (Grades do not match average or above-average I.Q. of the child.)
- Develop negative attitude and behavior problems due to inadequate academic performance.
  (Becomes a "problem child" or disruptive in the classroom.)
- Act out or are extremely shy and withdrawn.
  (Child is disruptive, unusually aggressive, or clowns in classroom; *or* child is painfully shy and quiet, does not call attention to himself, and has few friends.)
- Have blood relatives (i.e., mother, father, siblings, cousins, aunts, and/or uncles) who also have inadequate language skills.

Adults
- Are high school dropouts.
- Hate to read; avoid reading whenever possible.
- Cannot fill out job application.
- Have employment problems due to inability to read.
- Have low self-esteem and lack self-confidence; hide deficiency.
- Never reach career or learning potential.

A good rule of thumb to follow when using the checklist is to pay attention to your initial response. Is it a deep breath followed by "Aha!"? You know your child better than anyone else. Do the characteristics sound familiar? What you suspect may be off base, or right on the mark. Either way your suspicions need to be validated and put to rest, once and for all.

WHY ARE EDUCATORS THE LAST TO KNOW?

Let's talk about educators and, specifically, teacher training. Fact: teacher training hasn't changed one bit since I graduated from college (1960) with a Nebraska teacher's certificate in hand. Teacher training begins and ends with an emphasis on rote learning or, as I see it, minutia. Our young, vivacious teachers are drowning in technique, factoids, and pop psychology, without the guidance necessary to recognize *differences* among students.

Most teachers are trained to meet the needs of 60 percent of their classroom student body. The remaining 40 percent of the class is split: 20 percent have some type of learning disability and 20 percent are classified as gifted. It's not the fault of these young teachers; they don't know any better. The real culprit lies with the teacher-training programs on the university level; they need a major overhaul.

From now on, I'm going to use a term to help you fine-tune your response to troubling aspects of your child's academic aptitude. (Likewise, if you are a dyslexic adult, it will help you get in touch with your own learning style.) Red Flag is the term I want you to register. Red Flags, which are triggered when your intuition tells you something's suspect, are reliable warnings. Examples are:

Red Flag: Your child is not reading along with all the other first-graders by the end of the school year.

Red Flag: Your first-grader, who was all enthused about school in September, is discouraged by May.

Red Flag: Your first-grader can say the alphabet aloud, but cannot identify or write the letters.

Red Flag: Your child is sick every Monday morning and hates going to school.

Red Flag: You, the parent, have to re-read your company manual at least 10 times before you get the point.

Red Flag: You don't take notes, you rely on your memory, and miss that important dinner with the boss!

Red Flag: Your friend tells you to turn right, and you turn left, everytime.

Red Flag: Your attention wanders from the printed page after five minutes of reading.

I think you get the idea.

THE NEXT IMPORTANT STEP—EVALUATION REQUEST

Now that you've come to a conclusion about the symptoms, how do you initiate the next step? You make arrangements for an educational evaluation. Sounds simple, but it's not.

I will take you through the second part of the process, step by step. Check off each step as it's accomplished and before you know it, the evaluation will be complete. The steps differ for children and adults, so we will cover the steps for children first.

THE REQUEST FOR A CHILD

Step 1. Go to your child's teacher. Share your concerns and ask for input. The teacher will coordinate your request for testing and the process will begin. In the event you receive a less-than-ideal response, go to Step 2.

Step 2. In writing, request an educational evaluation for your child. Make five copies. Hand deliver or mail one copy to each of the following: the homeroom teacher, counselor, principal, and superintendent. Keep one copy for yourself.

Here is a sample of the letter you want to send:

Date

Name of Principal
Name of School
Address of School

Dear (Principal):

I am the parent of (name of child). My child is having problems with his schoolwork. Please arrange an individual, educational assessment to see if he has a handicap and needs special services. Also, please tell me in writing who will give the assessment, what tests will be used, and what date the assessment will be administered.

Thank you for your attention to my request. I look forward to hearing from you within five school days of the date you receive this letter.

Sincerely,

(Your name)
(Your address)
(Your telephone number)

Step 3. Usually, within 5 to 10 days from the date of your initial request, you will be contacted by the principal or a staff person to set up the evaluation process. Release forms will be sent to you for you to sign. If you are not contacted within 10 days, follow up by phone or in person, and ask the principal about the status of your request. Emphasize the urgency of this matter.

Step 4. Contact your state education agency. (See the appendices for state listings.) Ask for the special education department and the person in charge of the dyslexia program. Tell that person you want information concerning (state) programs and services available for your child.

Step 5. Contact your state's Client Assistance Agency. (See the appendices for state listings.) Ask for literature and manuals regarding education for handicapped children.

Step 6. Discuss what you are doing with your child and why. Be up front and honest. Say, "I know you are working as hard as you can. But your grades don't reflect all your effort. We need to pin down the problem so you can be the best student possible."

A word to the wise about two classifications mentioned above: one is "special education"; the other is "handicapped." Do not be offended or put off by these terms. Because of state requirements, services rendered must be justified. In other words, funding for special programs often originates in the special education division of education departments. Learning disabilities, because of semantics (or wording) fall under the heading of "handicapping conditions."

Some parents fear labeling their child, so they avoid all mention of their child's learning problems. Rest assured, your child *will* be labeled as he stumbles through the educational system.

Wouldn't you prefer to have a handle on the problem from the start, to be in charge of what happens next so your child isn't labeled lazy or uncooperative?

OTHER TESTING RESOURCES FOR CHILDREN:
- Easter Seal Society
- Community mental health agencies
- University-affiliated children's hospitals
- Private (Look in the yellow pages under Educational Associations, Educational Consultants, or Educational Diagnosticians.)

TO REVIEW
1. Evaluation request (in writing)
2. Begin file of information resources and phone numbers; get the name and telephone number of every contact.
3. Talk openly with your child about the process.

THE REQUEST FOR A COLLEGE STUDENT
Contact the dean of special services at your local college or university. Testing arrangements are made at low cost for enrolled students.

(Read chapter 8 for a detailed discussion of the type of college program you want and how to get it.)

THE REQUEST FOR AN ADULT
Step 1. Contact your state's Vocational Rehabilitation Commission(VRC). (See the appendices for state listings.) The state office can refer you to the nearest area office.

Step 2. Make an appointment with the VRC office to see if you are eligible for services. If eligible, there will be either no charge or a minimal charge for testing.

Step 3. If you are ineligible for services, contact your county's Health and Human Services Bureau and ask for a list of local testing resources.

Step 4. Some community colleges and universities will share their resources for testing; others only serve enrolled students. It's worth a phone call to the department of special services to ask.

Step 5. Contact your local library. Libraries are anxious to assist the public, especially those with reading difficulties. Ask the librarian for a listing of potential testing resources.

Step 6. Contact your city information and referral service or the local United Way office. They each have valuable resource contacts.

OTHER TESTING RESOURCES FOR ADULTS
- Adult Education/Literacy Councils
- Community mental health agencies
- Private diagnosticians who specialize in evaluating adults with learning disabilities (See the yellow pages under Educational Associations, Educational Consultants, or Educational Diagnosticians.)

TO REVIEW
1. Start a file and keep the name of the person, agency, and phone number for each contact.
2. Become best friends with your local librarian (an invaluable resource, especially when you share objectives in this case).
3. If you become a state rehabilitation client, ask about other available services.

Remember: Keep copies of every document, paper, or piece of correspondence that crosses between you and the school or you and the provider. Make sure the information is dated and signed by a contact person. Careful record keeping will serve you well in the event you are asked to prove promises made.

Remember: Verbal promises don't count. Make sure *everything* promised or discussed is verified in writing and signed. Schools, agencies, and institutions live by the written word and cannot keep up with client requests just by verbal communication.

THE BUCK STOPS HERE
Recently, I attended a conference sponsored by the National Center for Learning Disabilities held at Southern Methodist

University in Dallas, Texas. One of the speakers was Lionel Meno, commissioner of the Texas State Board of Education. When Dr. Meno discussed the crisis in education, he addressed one particular issue that affirmed my belief concerning responsibility. Dr. Meno said, "It is up to the parent to make sure the school does what it is supposed to do."

In other words, don't depend on the school to take the initiative when it comes to identifying your child's learning problems. You take the initiative. You steer your own ship. (For adult dyslexics, you must initiate your contacts as well. State agencies will not send a sheriff's posse to find you.)

How to Cut Through the Red Tape
1. Be single-minded.
2. Be firm.
3. Be knowledgeable.

Above all, you must know your rights. Know your child's rights, your rights as a parent, your rights as an individual. The next chapter will spell out the legal rights of citizens of the United States regarding disabilities, and outline those that specifically pertain to dyslexia.

BOOKS OF INTEREST

Blue, Rose. *Me and Einstein: Breaking Through the Reading Barrier.* New York: Human Sciences Press, Inc., 1985.

This book is an oldie but a goodie. Illustrated text for children between the ages of 8 and 12. Available from Human Sciences Press: 1-800-221-9369.

Cordoni, Barbara. *Living With a Learning Disability.* Carbondale: Southern Illinois University Press, 1990.

Replete with alternative methods of teaching academic skills. Adaptations for educating, communicating with, and parenting the learning-disabled child.

Huston, Anne Marshall. *Understanding Dyslexia.* New York: Madison Books, 1992.

Helps parents better understand the nature of dyslexia as a legitimate disability. Explains the difficult problems that accompany dyslexia.

Levinson, Harold, M.D. and Addie Sanders. *Turning Around the Upside Down Kids: Helping Dyslexic Kids Overcome Their Disorder.* New York: M. Evans and Company, 1992.

Provides comprehensive understanding of all the symptoms and helpful therapies characterizing dyslexia and dyslexics.

Osmond, John. *The Reality of Dyslexia.* Cambridge, MA: Brookline Books, 1994.

A father's personal account of his dyslexic son's progress and his own as a parent. Includes detailed case studies, as told by the people involved and focuses on the experience of dyslexics and their families.

Rosner, Jerome. *Helping Children Overcome Learning Difficulties.* New York: Walker and Co., 1993.

Provides parents, teachers, and others with a guide and reference to a prescriptive approach tailored to each child's needs. New information about dyslexia with a detailed plan parents can use to help their children.

3 KNOWING YOUR LEGAL RIGHTS

The Education for All Handicapped Children Act of 1975 (Public Law 94-142) is the federal law that guarantees every handicapped child between the ages of 3 and 21 a free, appropriate public education. As recently as 1970, 48 states and the District of Columbia had statutes on the books that excluded physically and mentally handicapped students from compulsory school attendance. Handicapped children were not a good educational investment, some argued, and therefore were not entitled to public support for their education.

WHAT PUBLIC LAW (P.L.) 94-142 SAYS

Every child, regardless of handicap, has the right to be educated and receive related services to meet his unique needs. The law provides that states may receive federal assistance for educating handicapped children and requires parents to be involved in making educational decisions for their handicapped children. Under state and federal law, public school districts are required to comply with the provisions of P.L. 94-142 whether they receive direct or indirect federal funds. The following passage from P.L. 94-142 spells out who is eligible for services under the heading of what constitutes "specific learning disability":

Specific learning disability means a disorder in one or more of the basic psychological processes involved in understanding or in using language, spoken or written, which may manifest itself in an imperfect ability to listen, think, speak, read, write, spell, or to do mathematical calculations. The term includes such conditions as perceptual handicaps, brain injury, minimal brain dysfunction, *dyslexia* [my italics], and developmental aphasia....

WHAT P.L. 94-142 PROVIDES

The federal mandate profiles the required steps for:

1. identifying handicapped children;
2. evaluating or assessing children;
3. developing an individual education plan (IEP) for each handicapped child before he receives special education;
4. deciding what special instruction and which services are to be provided;
5. deciding how handicapped children are to be placed;
6. maintaining education records and files for children in special education; and
7. hearings and appeals for complaints or grievances.

HOW P.L. 94-142 AFFECTS DYSLEXIC CHILDREN

Because "learning disability" is a broad umbrella term, and because who might be "handicapped" is equally vague, it is especially important to note the inclusion of dyslexia in the target population affected by P.L. 94-142.

Yet, even with federal legislation in place, some schools refused to comply with P.L.92-142 or limited services to the learning disabled, including dyslexics, who were two years or more behind their grade levels. This left many dyslexic students identified, but unserved and excluded, which meant they had to fend for themselves in the regular classroom, or they dropped out of school rather than continuing to face failure. Then, in 1976, the Rehabilitation Act of 1973, Section 504 (P.L. 93-112) was amended to ensure schools' compliance with P.L. 94-142.

UNDERSTANDING SECTION 504

Section 504 is a civil rights amendment that prohibits discrimination on the basis of handicap. The term "handicapped" covers those individuals with specific learning disabilities, including dyslexia. In 1976, an executive order amended Section 504 and subparts D and E of 504 were then consistent with P.L. 94-142.

Section 504 says: "No otherwise qualified handicapped individual in the United States...shall solely by reason of his handicap, be excluded from the participation in, be denied the benefits of, or be subjected to discrimination under any program or activity receiving federal financial assistance."

What about separate programs for dyslexic students? Schools cannot deny an individual with a disability participation in its regular program. Unfortunately, some schools just don't get it. Placing dyslexic students in special programs designed for the severely mentally retarded is a commonly occurring example.

For more complete information regarding Section 504 of the Rehabilitation Act of 1973, contact your local civil rights office by calling 1-800-368-1019, or writing to:

Office For Civil Rights
Cohen Building, #5039
330 Independence Avenue, SW
Washington, DC 20201

THE BENEFITS OF THE INDIVIDUALS WITH DISABILITIES EDUCATION ACT OF 1990 (AMENDED BY P.L. 101-476)

The Individuals with Disabilities Education Act (IDEA) is a fabulous, detailed document describing just about everything you'd ever want to know concerning the state's responsibility for children and youth with disabilities. IDEA addresses the problem of "exclusion" by stating that the "special educational needs of more than 8 million children with disabilities in the United States...are not being met." IDEA goes on to say, "It is in the national interest that the federal government assist state and local efforts to provide programs to meet the educational needs of children with disabilities in order to assure equal protection of the law."

What makes IDEA so important is the financial commitment of the federal government to the individual states. Before IDEA, the mandated programs floundered because of lack of funding. Now that the money is appropriated and available for the asking, there is absolutely no excuse for there to be a lack of special services available for your dyslexic child.

The National Information Center for Children and Youth with Disabilities (NICHCY) distributes several publications you must have. One is *Questions and Answers About the Individuals with Disabilities Education Act (IDEA)* (Vol. III, No. 2, 1993). The other is *The Education of Children and Youth with Special Needs: What Do the Laws Say?* (Vol. I, No. 1, 1991). Single copies are free. To order these materials, contact:

National Information Center for Children
and Youth with Disabilities
P.O. Box 1492
Washington, DC 20013-1492
1-800-695-0285

State Law for School-Age Children

Each state operates under a federal mandate to comply with P.L. 94-142 and Section 504. In case of conflict, the federal law must always be obeyed with no exceptions. Ever.

In Texas, for example, House Bill (H.B.)157 legislates a statewide dyslexia program in response to the federal mandate. Passing H.B. 157 was a hard-fought battle, with many special interest groups challenging the move. However, in 1985, the bill passed and the Texas Education Agency was assigned responsibility for implementing the program.

The problem in Texas, as in most other states, is not lack of intent, rather, it is the lack of program consistency from district to district. More confusing is the lack of consistency within the same district. Case in point: The Texas Dyslexia Mandate was seriously challenged by parents in 1990, unanimously re-affirmed by the legislature with rules defining the law, *and* still is not delivered in a consistent manner throughout the state.

The good news is this: other states (Louisiana, Mississippi, and California) have followed Texas' lead in establishing mandated dyslexia programs modeled after H.B. 157. The raised awareness of the need for specific guidelines in state and local legislation is catching on. Without a doubt, the winning combination ensuring implementation of the legislative effort is parental pressure and continued monitoring of the results. Keep reading, and you will have all the tools necessary to become an informed, involved citizen, and champion of your child's best interest.

LOCAL IMPLEMENTATION OF FEDERAL AND STATE LAW

All local school districts are required to follow state and federal regulations concerning requests for educational evaluation. If your child is in a small private school and diagnostic services are not available, you can go to the public school district in which you reside and request the evaluation. As a resident citizen and taxpayer in the district, your child is entitled to testing services at no charge.

If you are challenged in your effort to obtain free testing, refer the administrator to Federal Regulation 300.128, Comment, which says: "The State is responsible for insuring that all handicapped children are identified, located, and evaluated, including children in all public and private agencies and institutions in the State." (Remember, all requests must be made in writing.)

If the public school district in which your child is enrolled cannot provide the service because there is no diagnostician available, then the school district must pay for a private evaluation. First check with your district's policy and follow their guidelines before making arrangements for private evaluation if you expect them to pay for it.

LEGAL RECOURSE

If you believe you are getting the runaround, or the response to your request for testing is less than adequate, contact your local Office For Civil Rights. Each office has a special division that oversees complaints by parents concerning a school district's lack of compliance with the law.

The Office For Civil Rights is not the last resort. There are lawyers who have expertise in the education of children and public law who are available to represent your case. An attorney will, of course, charge a consultation fee to meet with you and discuss your case. However, the school district may be ordered to pay this fee if you win the case. When seeking legal counsel, ask the magic question: How many cases of this nature have you won and what was the outcome?

More and more parents are challenging the status quo. A landmark decision concerning the individual rights of dyslexic students in the United States was recently made by the Supreme Court. The decision is just one example that helps define the state's responsibility with regard to federal requirements.

THE SUPREME COURT DECISION

"A State shall not be immune...from suit in Federal court for a violation of this Act." (Section 1403(a), IDEA, October 30, 1990.)

In 1986 the parents of a learning-disabled child sued the Florence County School District in South Carolina (*Carter v. Florence County School District Four*), alleging that the school district breached its statutory duty to provide their child with a free, appropriate public education. The parents requested reimbursement for the tuition costs of a private school in which they unilaterally placed the child.

The district court ordered the public school district to reimburse the parents in the sum of $35,716.11, plus prejudgment interest. The school district appealed and the case found its way to the U.S. Court of Appeals in 1991 where it was heard and affirmed with the following disposition: "...we simply cannot convert state approval of a parent's private school placement of a handicapped child into a condition for reimbursement...when a state has defaulted on its statutory obligations."

In October 1993, the Supreme Court heard the case and upheld the lower court decision in a brief written by Justice Sandra Day O'Connor.

As you see, the legal process is not swift. It took years in court to challenge the public school system and win. Thanks to this student's parents, one more step in the right direction was taken for dyslexic students. By the way, this dyslexic South Carolina student is now in postsecondary technical school continuing her education.

YOUR LEGAL RIGHTS

It is especially helpful to know your legal rights. The following list spells out basic rights concerning your handicapped child's evaluation, records, and individualized education plan (I.E.P.). The RIGHT to know what the policies are regarding storage, retention, or destruction of records on your child and to review and inspect these records.

The RIGHT to know who else, besides yourself, can inspect these records and to know all the places where information on your child is stored.

The RIGHT to have a representative of your chioce inspect and interpret your child's records in lay language.

The RIGHT to disallow anyone other than officials and agents of the public agency (the school district, for example), who could use the information, to inspect your child's records until your permission to do so is granted.

The RIGHT to request, when information is no longer needed for storage or use by the public agency, that it be destroyed except for very basic information that may be required later, e.g., social security benefits, etc.

The RIGHT to be notified in advance of meetings pertaining to your child and to expect understandable language presentations in your native tongue at such meetings and all communications to you in your native tongue.

The RIGHT to have your child tested in his native tongue.

The RIGHT to have an interpreter at a meeting when language may be a barrier to understanding.

The RIGHT to have an interdisciplinary team evaluate your child.

The RIGHT to have an annual review of your child's educational program and to have educational placement for your child made by a team of people.

The RIGHT to bring someone of your choice to all meetings to assist you.

The RIGHT to have your child educated when and where possible in a program as close as possible to your home.

The RIGHT to a series of "related" services that may include such things as transportation, counseling, medical services, etc., which are written into the individualized education plan (IEP) and are free to the child and family.

The RIGHT to a program tailored to your child's needs, which includes services such as physical education, recreation, career and vocational education, etc.

The RIGHT to have your child, when feasible, placed in the "least restrictive environment," that is, to be placed with non-handicapped children.

The RIGHT to have your child evaluated on a series of tests that not only confirm that a handicapping condition exists, but that help explain why and what can be done about it.

The RIGHT to refer your own child for education under the provision of P.L. 94-142 and to challenge any decision made regarding the identification, placement, and education of your child.

The RIGHT to have tests used with your child that are not racially or culturally discriminating.

The RIGHT to have an individualized education plan (IEP) written for your child within 30 calendar days after he has been diagnosed as handicapped by the evaluation team.

The RIGHT to have your child tested in all areas related to the suspected disability (including, when appropriate, health, vision, hearing, social and emotional status, general intelligence, academic performance, communicative status, and motor abilities) and to have a re-evaluation every three years.

The RIGHT to participate in all meetings regarding the development, revision and review of the IEP for your child and to have an IEP include various alternative placements.

The RIGHT to agree or disagree with ideas concerning educational plans for your child and not to be bound by what the public agency can offer in services that are needed but to focus on what your child needs.

The RIGHT for a fully paid private school placement if referred to such a setting because it is deemed in your child's best interest.

(The above legal rights are taken from Federal Register, Vol. 42, No. 163, August 23, 1977 and the Family Education Rights and Privacy Act.)

WHAT ABOUT RIGHTS FOR ADULT DYSLEXICS?

In July 1990, Congress passed the Americans with Disabilities Act (P.L. 101-336). The enactment created much rejoicing because it gives Americans with disabilities an equal opportunity to live and work like everyone else. The definition of an individual with a disability is restricted to those with "physical or mental impairments," which include a specific learning disability or dyslexia.

According to the Americans with Disabilities Act (ADA), "A qualified individual with a disability is a person who meets legitimate skill, experience, or education, or other requirements of an employment position that he holds or seeks, and who can perform the 'essential functions' of the position with or without reasonable accommodation."

Reasonable accommodations may include:

1. Adjusting work schedules
2. Acquiring or modifying equipment
3. Modifying examinations, training, or other programs
4. Providing qualified readers or interpreters

All accommodations are considered case by case so as to not inflict undue hardship on the employer. What the new law provides is better access for the handicapped, including dyslexics, to jobs, public accommodations, government services, public transportation, and telecommunications systems.

Implementation of the ADA is mandatory for each state and guidelines for employer accommodations are available from the Equal Employment Opportunity Commission (EEOC). You can get a free copy of regulations, accessibility, and the law from:

Equal Employment Opportunity Commission
1801 L Street, NW
Washington, DC 20507
1-800-669-EEOC (publications)

Ready? Now that you are armed with basic legal rights information, we'll move to the educational evaluation process. In the next chapter, the evaluation process is outlined with easy-to-follow steps that will help familiarize you with the formal aspects of assessment.

BOOKS OF INTEREST

Ballard, Joseph and others. *P. L. 94-142, Section 504, and P. L. 99-457—Understanding What They Are and Are Not*. Reston, VA: The Council for Exceptional Children, 1990.

Reflects legislative changes affecting the education of disabled children. Answers questions about rights, fiscal policy, and management. Order from: Council for Exceptional Children, Department K4012, 1920 Association Drive, Reston, VA 22091-1589.

Beckman, Paula J. and Gayle Beckman Boyes. *Deciphering the System: A Guide for Families of Young Children with Disabilities.* Cambridge, MA: Brookline Books, 1993.

Primarily addresses the needs of young children with disabilities who are between birth and five years of age. Provides basic information about recent legislation and service providers. Order from: Brookline Books, P.O. Box, 1046, Cambridge, MA 02238.

Bogin, Matthew B. and Beth Goodwin. *Representing Learning Disabled Children: A Manual for Attorneys.* Washington: American Bar Association, National Resource Center for Child Advocacy and Protection, 1985.

Emphasizes the representation of children with learning problems who have not yet received the services to which they are entitled and are not yet in the court system. Order from: NCLD, 381 Park Avenue S., #1420, New York, NY 10016.

McGee, Judge Thomas P. and John B. Sikorski M.D. *Learning Disabilities and the Juvenile Justice System—A Bench Book for Juvenile and Family Court Judges. Juvenile and Family Court Journal/*Vol. 37, No. 3, 1986.

Provides information necessary to deal with the rights of children with learning disabilities who are already before the courts for reasons other than their learning disabilities. Order from: National Council of Juvenile and Family Court Judges, P.O. Box 8970, Reno, NV 89507.

4 THE
EDUCATIONAL
EVALUATION

Where do you start? The best place to start is right where you are. If your child is enrolled in a public school, like the majority of students, the nearest resource is your own school. For those enrolled in private schools, the same resource is available. If your child's private school does not offer testing, you have the right to request the testing resources of the public school district in which you live. If they do not provide testing services, but instead subcontract services through an independent testing resource, you have the right to request such services. First check with your school district's specific guidelines, then follow the request-for-evaluation steps outlined in chapter 2.

Who do you ask? Ask the child's teacher first. If the teacher doesn't know, ask the principal. If the principal doesn't know, call the superintendent's office and ask for the Special Education Department. If they don't know, and make no effort to find out, stop being polite and whip out your Client Advocacy and Education Agency booklets and start quoting. Usually you won't have to go to such extremes, but it's been known to happen.

Generally, the request can be handled swiftly and

through the channels described in chapter 2. You do not have to present a treatise on why you are requesting the educational evaluation. Such requests are not spur-of-the-moment or frivolous concoctions. The red flags have been noticeable for a long time. Simply put, you've decided to act.

A PARENT'S DILEMMA

To put your situation in perspective, consider the following letter from a frustrated Kansas parent:

Sirs:

We have a daughter, Becky, who is in the sixth grade and reading at third-grade level. We have gone through so much to get help for her and seem to be getting nowhere. The school tells us she will outgrow her problems. Meanwhile, Becky struggles for hours on her homework and still fails.

We are afraid Becky is losing heart. We appreciate any help that we could get...any school that could help, etc. We want to help Becky and keep running into walls....

Sincerely,

A Concerned Parent

My advice to this parent: Don't waste another minute! Initiate the first step by officially requesting an educational evaluation. Follow the steps outlined in chapter 2. Then, start collecting the legal rights material itemized in chapter 3. Don't forget—it's all free.

You go to bat for your child. If you don't, *no one* else will.

WHERE TO GO FOR TESTING?

The majority of educational evaluations are done on site. This means the testing professional(s) will come to your child's school or a nearby location, such as the district's special education building or the administration office. Otherwise the testing facility can be mutually agreed upon.

How much do you pay? Nothing. The school district in which you reside provides the service. Proof of residence may be required.

Proof of residence can include:
1. Property tax statement.
2. Affidavit of residence.
3. Enrollment of your child in school district (public or private).

If you decide to use a private resource, and pay for the testing yourself, the cost can range from $350 to $750. Most educational evaluations are not covered by health insurance. However, check with your insurance carrier first to make sure. Now, let's take a look at the steps leading up to the actual testing process.

THE FIRST STEP

What helps us understand the unfamiliar and reach a comfort level is asking questions and receiving answers. The best way to keep track of the answers is to take copious notes or to simply tape record the conversation. Remember, this is serious business. You want to understand everything you agree to when signing on the dotted line.

WHAT KIND OF QUESTIONS DO YOU ASK?

Here is a sample list:
1. What tests will be given?
2. Why are those tests chosen for the student?
3. How will the tests be given?
4. What are they supposed to show?
5. How will the results be reported?
6. When will the tests be administered and how soon afterward will results be available?

THE EVALUATION TEAM'S QUALIFICATIONS

The qualification requirements for evaluation vary from state to state. In some states, the screening test for dyslexia may be administered by the student's classroom teacher. The student then may be referred to a remedial program and receive special support in the regular classroom. In other states, the educational evaluation is administered by a testing specialist and includes representatives from interdisciplinary or multidisciplinary disciplines. Don't let the terminology throw you. Basically, the team members include people already familiar to you, joined by professionals representing related or overlapping specialties.

The qualification requirements of the testing specialist also vary from state to state. The minimum credentials should include a bachelor's degree from an accredited university with appropriate certification, or endorsement and/or licensure. Ask about the evaluator's credentials and professional affiliation with such organizations as the (state) Educational Diagnostician's Association.

The remaining team members may include professionals with the following titles:

1. Resource or special education teacher, diagnostician.
2. Language therapist, speech therapist, reading specialist.
3. School administrator (principal), special education consultant, special program consultant.
4. Dyslexia designee, content mastery teacher, 504 coordinator.
5. Others: psychologist, physician, teacher, counselor.

THE EVALUATION

To help you better understand the testing process, I have outlined a description of procedures and instruments that may be selected. Since the state is only required to test in the area of suspected disability, not all of the tests listed may be used. However, if you know what the administered instruments actually assess, you'll be more comfortable when discussing the results.

Physical Exam

A physical exam, including auditory and visual evaluation is the first step in the actual evaluation process. In most cases, the parent is responsible for providing the general physical history report. The purpose of the physical exam is to rule out brain injury, disease, or surgery as the cause or origin of a learning disability. The school usually has qualified personnel available to perform the hearing and vision portions.

Family History

This portion can help trace the presence of other family members who have experienced problems with reading, writing, or spelling and/or unspecified poor academic performance. The significance of such observations is to help show the genetic component of dyslexia or other learning disabilities.

Oral Language Tests

The following assess receptive and expressive language skills:
(CELF-R)—Clinical Evaluation of Language Function
(TOLD-2)—Test of Language Development
(TOAL)—Test of Adolescent Language

I.Q. Score

Intelligence tests are designed to measure one's ability to learn. Most tests are standardized, based on responses from a sample of the general population, covering a range of ages and abilities. Often this score has little bearing on the student's true ability to learn or perform tasks. Remember, an intelligence test must never be used as the sole determinant of placement.

Examples of I.Q. tests include:

- Wechsler Intelligence Scales for Children (WISC-III)
- Stanford-Binet Intelligence Scale
- Kaufman Assessment Battery for Children (KABC)
- Wechsler Adult Intelligence Scale (WAIS-R)
- Wechsler Preschool & Primary Scale of Intelligence (WPPSI-R)
- Nonverbal I.Q. test—Test of Nonverbal Intelligence (TONI-2)

Achievement Tests

Achievement tests are designed to assess what a student has learned in relation to other students of the same age and grade level. The tests measure specific types of achievement in academic fields such as math, reading, language, and science. The newer, revised achievement tests consist of multidimensional subtests that measure the ability to read words in context or to comprehend the meaning of what is read.

Examples of achievement tests include:

- Wide Range Achievement Test-3 (WRAT-R)
- Woodcock-Johnson-R
- Wechsler Individual Achievement Test (WIAT)
- Test of Academic Achievement Skills—Reading, Arithmetic, and Spelling (TAAS-RAS)
- Diagnostic Achievement Battery-2 (DAB-2)

These tests are administered individually and are reliable tools for diagnosing learning disabilities when used in combination with other standard tests.

Reading Achievement Tests

A measure of reading comprehension is important to the overall diagnostic process. Obviously reading comprehension cannot be assessed if the student can't read or is too young to read. However, for the older student who is having trouble with reading comprehension, or reading in general, such tests are entirely appropriate.

Examples of reading achievement tests include:

- Gates-MacGinitie—tests reading comprehension and vocabulary achievement.
- Gray Oral Reading Test—diagnostic test that gives grade/age equivalency.
- Spadafore Diagnostic Reading Test—provides comprehensive assessment of reading skills.

Written Language Achievement Tests

A measure of written language ability is also an important element of the testing process because expressing thoughts on paper coherently requires reading, spelling, and organizational skills. If there is an age/grade discrepancy, the written language test will determine the variance.

Examples of Written Language Tests include:

- **(TOWL-2)**—Test of Written Language measures a student's strengths and weaknesses in writing.
- **(WLA)**—Written Language Assessment offers direct assessment of written language through an evaluation of writing samples.

Handwriting Assessments

- **(CHES)**—The Children's Handwriting Evaluation System tests handwriting capabilities for rate and legibility (grades 1–12).
- **(DHA)**—The Denver Handwriting Analysis is an informal cursive handwriting evaluation that provides a remedial checklist.

Please note: All of these standard tests are not the only instruments available, but can serve as a source of information about the type of testing that may be administered.

TEACHER INTERVIEW

Observation of student's classroom performance, participation, and ability to attend to tasks (follow directions) is another part of the evaluation process that is often mentioned and is a key component of the overall assessment.

Response is given by a third party close to the student (i.e., teacher, counselor, etc.). The validity of these questionnaires depends on the interviewer's objectivity and attitude toward the student.

Beware of a long list of complaints about the student. Usually this means the person presenting the information has a poor understanding of the differences between children, especially behavioral differences derived from learning differences. Even though teachers are professionals by designation, they are human in nature. If the teacher has nothing positive to say about the student, request an independent assessment interview.

BASIC BATTERY OVERVIEW

The handwriting and oral language tests are often, but not always, part of the achievement battery. These two tests are intended to supplement the more extensive achievement test battery (i.e., the WRAT-R, WIAT, TAAS-RAS). The significant scores show discrepancies (or variance) between performance and I.Q.

For example, if your child has average or above average intelligence, is in the sixth grade, and his reading comprehension is at a second- or third-grade level, that is not normal. Furthermore, if we are addressing the issue of dyslexia, the performance gap shrinks as the student progresses through the educational system. The end result is an eighteen-year-old senior who talks a good game, but is functionally illiterate.

Remember, one score or one test by itself does not give the complete picture, which is why dyslexia is often overlooked. Therein lies the problem and the rationale for using the battery of evaluation instruments reviewed above.

PERSONALITY TESTS

What about personality tests? Personality tests tend to be controversial because they carry the stigma of "crazy" or "bad" and are subjective in interpretation. The validity of such tests are the subject of controversy among psychologists. Also, without parents' receiving prior notice and thus the opportunity to object, personality tests may not be used.

Whether such a test is included depends on the use of results. If a personality test is recommended, don't be afraid to question the purpose and relevance. Ask about the qualifications of the examiner (i.e., certification, licensure, and professional affiliations).

A FINAL SUGGESTION

The Connors Rating Scale is an example of a simple, one-page assessment you may request. The results will rule out or identify Attention Deficit Hyperactivity Disorder (ADHD), which sometimes accompanies dyslexia. ADHD is another topic with literature available describing symptoms and practical help for the disorder.

EVALUATIONS FOR COLLEGE STUDENTS AND ADULTS

The testing devices for both college students and adults may vary from the battery listed above, but the program is basically the same. The only difference may be the inclusion of personal interest surveys, vocational preference exams, and aptitude testing.

REVIEWING THE EVALUATION RESULTS

Who is present?

Generally speaking, those who attend the review of results include:

1. The individual who has been evaluated (for children in middle school or high school).
2. The parent or guardian (if subject is under age 18).
3. The examiner.
4. School counselor, principal, and teacher(s).
5. Coordinator/contact person.
6. Dyslexia designee (a professional who has expertise in orchestrating remedial services, related services, and regular classroom activities for the dyslexic student).

The Meeting

The name of the meeting differs from state to state, but may generally fall under one of the following acronyms:

1. ARD (Admission, Review, and Dismissal) Committee

2. IEP (Individualized Education Plan) Meeting

3. MOT (Multidisciplinary Team) Meeting

Schools are advised by attorneys to tape record the proceedings at these meetings. I advise you to do the same. Also, if you are not entirely comfortable representing your child or yourself, you can ask for advocacy assistance from the ombudsman program (call the school administration office) or local support group. (See chapter 10 for details about area support groups.)

The examiner will explain the test results and significance of scoring in relation to the individual's academic performance. If the explanation is confusing, don't pretend to understand. Speak up. Ask the person who gives the readout to go over the explanation again. The bottom line is this: you need to be comfortable with the explanation in order to understand what is normal and what is abnormal.

Pay particular attention to reading comprehension; it should be close to your child's age and grade level; if not, this is a red flag. If the scoring scale is even, then dips significantly low in the area of written language skills, you have another red flag. If the achievement scores do not correspond to the I.Q. score, it's one more red flag.

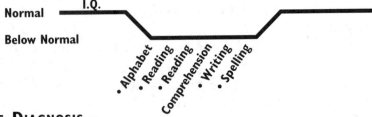

THE DIAGNOSIS

The diagnosis can be illuminating or can leave you more confused than ever. Test results vary from vague, rambling narratives to single-line descriptions. Because there are no common parameters, the diagnosis from one state may not be the same as that from another state. Most states use the term "severe discrepancy" in their diagnosis; this lets everyone off the hook without naming the problem.

When you hear or read "severe discrepancy," it is time to ask, "Is my child dyslexic?" Don't be surprised if the evaluator says, "Off the record, he is. However, our school district does not use the term 'dyslexia' in diagnostic procedures."

Other descriptive diagnoses may be:

1. Developmental disorder not otherwise specified.
2. Specific developmental disorder not otherwise specified.
3. Academic skills disorder.
4. Specific language learning disability.
5. Developmental reading disorder.
6. Developmental dyslexia.
7. Specific language impairment.
8. Unspecified delay in development. (This one is a big cop-out!)

Here's the bottom line: specific dyslexia involves basic problems in learning the alphabet and its phonic properties; in word recognition, reading, reading comprehension, writing, copying, and spelling. The term "specific" is used to establish the fact that the child does not have mental retardation, brain damage, or primary emotional or mental problems. This means the family and home environment did not cause the disability nor is it the result of faulty training at school.

HOW ELIGIBILITY FOR SERVICES IS DETERMINED

The most popular criteria used by school districts to determine eligibility for special services is the "severe discrepancy" policy. What constitutes "severe discrepancy"?

The rule óf thumb for most states is that a discrepancy of 15 points between the full scale I.Q. score (ability) and the standard reading score (achievement) must be established in determining the existence of a specific learning disability. (A few states require a 22-point discrepancy to determine eligibility.)

Two other outdated but prevailing policies for determining severe discrepancy are:

1. The student's performance is two years behind grade/age level.
2. Remediation and/or related services provided only when the student is failing in all subjects.

Severe discrepancy is not limited to one area, but can include a discrepancy between achievement and intellectual ability in one or more of the following areas:

1. Oral expression
2. Listening comprehension
3. Written expression
4. Basic reading skill
5. Reading comprehension
6. Mathematics calculation
7. Mathematics reasoning

What happens if test results *do not* demonstrate a severe discrepancy, according to your state's requirement for establishing presence of a specific learning disability (dyslexia)? This does not mean your child is not eligible for services.

Remember, the consensus as to what constitutes a severe discrepancy is arguable between experts and varies from state to state. This is why it is important to use the multidisciplinary team approach, including classroom teacher observation, parental input, family history, and the formal educational evaluation instruments. This approach maximizes the opportunity to identify any learning difficulties.

SPECIAL ED OR NOT?

Testing will result in one of two outcomes. Your child will or will not be eligible for services under special education guidelines. Just because the child isn't eligible for special education doesn't mean he is ineligible for special services, remediation, or accommodation.

In fact, most experts *do not* necessarily recommend special education placement for dyslexics. The objection stems from some school district's practice of lumping all handicapped students in a single resource room. A major mistake for schools is refusing to place a learning-disabled child in an appropriate environment that is the least restrictive.

Lack of staff or facilities also does not excuse the school from providing the appropriate remedial services required by the state's handicapped mandate or covered by the Rehabilitation Act, Section 504. There is *no cap* on the number of children with specific learning disabilities to be served.

HOW TO RESPOND IF THE SCHOOL GIVES YOU A HARD TIME

Let's role-play for a moment and pretend the conversation between the counselor and parent, Mrs. Jones, in this case, goes like any one of the following exchanges.

Scenario #1

Counselor: Yes, Mrs. Jones, your child has a problem, but doesn't meet the district (or state) requirement for special services.

Mrs. Jones: Why not?

Counselor: Because, Mrs. Jones, the discrepancy between Johnny's I.Q. score and his achievement score is less than the state requirement for services; therefore, Johnny is not eligible for special education or any other adaptation.

Mrs. Jones: A single score cannot be used as the sole criterion for exempting a student from services.

Scenario #2

Counselor: Mrs. Jones, we don't have the funding to accommodate your child.

Mrs. Jones: Lack of funding does not exempt the school district from providing necessary services.

Scenario #3

Counselor: Mrs. Jones, we don't have a program in place to help your child.

Mrs. Jones: What does this mean?

Counselor: You will have to find a tutor or someone who has expertise in working with dyslexics.

Mrs. Jones: According to P.L. 94-142 and Section 504, if the district cannot accommodate my child, then the district must pay for my child's remediation.

Counselor: We don't have funding for such accommodation.

Mrs. Jones: Allocation for funding is no excuse for non-compliance with P.L. 94-142.

Scenario #4

Counselor: Mrs. Jones, dyslexia is a medical problem and must be treated by a medical doctor.

Mrs. Jones: According to P.L. 94-142 and Section 504, dyslexia is specifically mentioned as a handicapping condition to be remediated by the school.

Scenario #5

Counselor: Mrs. Jones, we can't find a thing wrong with Johnny; he appears to be on task. [Even though he is failing!]
Mrs. Jones: I would appreciate copies of the testing so I can arrange an independent review of the information.
Counselor: We can't give you that information.
Mrs. Jones: I have the right, according to "Procedural Safeguards," P.L. 94-142, to see my child's records.

THE INDIVIDUALIZED EDUCATION PLAN (IEP)

Just exactly what is the IEP? The Individualized Education Plan (IEP) is probably the most important document you will receive. Within its pages are the steps the school will use to implement a program of remediation and special services for your child.

Development of the Individualized Education Plan for a student should be in writing and include:

1. The IEP team members' names and phone numbers.
2. A statement of the student's present levels of educational performance.
3. Specific educational goals and objectives.
   • Annual goals
   • Short-term objectives
4. An outline of specially designed instructional program and any related services. Also, specialized services, materials, and equipment if so required.
5. The services needed by your child, including frequency and amount of time.
6. Acknowledgment of the need for regular program participation, with the least restrictive environment clause.
7. Parental input (a *must* for any successful plan).

Remember, do not settle for vague terminology such as "help when the student needs it." This is a sure-fire way to be right back where you were before the testing. Ownership of who is responsible for what makes the all the difference in the world.

QUESTIONS TO ASK

1. When does the IEP start?
2. What are the responsibilities of the student, teacher(s), parents, and others?
3. Who will be coordinator/liaison between the student and the teacher and the parent and the teacher?
3. How will the program be monitored?
4. How will success or modifications be determined?
5. What is the time line for bench marks (determining improvement)?

Remember, if you are not satisfied with the IEP, *don't sign it.*

KEEPING TRACK OF PAPERWORK

Purchase a binder with rings and pockets. Keep every piece of correspondence and scrap of paper you write information on. If you aren't quite sure why you have a name and number, keep it anyway. Record all phone numbers and names of contacts; date all material.

Start with the Request for Evaluation letter (see chapter 2 for the sample) and keep going. (The list works for parents, a college student, or an adult. The steps are basically the same, except for steps 7, 8, and 9, which apply to elementary and high school students only.)

Use the checklist below to keep track of your personal agenda.

EVALUATION CHECKLIST

1. ____Made initial contact with resource (i.e., teacher, agency, private testing facility) on (date).
   Contact name: _____
   Contact's telephone number: _____
2. ____Mailed written request for evaluation on (date).
   ____Copies attached.
3. ____Received written confirmation of testing to be done on (date).
   ____Copies attached.
4. ____Met with coordinator to ask questions and outline plan for evaluation on (date).
   Coordinator's name: _____
   Coordinator's telephone number: _____

____Copies of notes/audio attached.
5. ____Signed release papers for permission to conduct evaluation and returned to teacher on (date).
____Copies attached.
6. ____Readout of evaluation on (date).
____Diagnosis established on (date).
____Referral received (if indicated).
____Copies attached.

The following are for elementary, middle, or high school students:

7. ____Admissions/Review/Dismissal meeting on (date).
____Notes/audio attached.
8. ____Individualized Educational Plan (IEP) developed on (date).
____Copies attached.
9. ____Six week follow-up on progress/adjustments needed on (date).
____Notes/audio attached.
10. ____Miscellaneous correspondence or notes attached.

OVERWHELMED?

Don't be. The checklist is simply a way for you to keep track of the process. Let the professionals do the work. The important thing is that you to feel comfortable with what is happening. If you don't understand, ask questions. If you disagree, speak up. If you are dissatisfied with the results or the readout, voice your complaint. The IEP cannot be implemented unless there is mutual agreement and consent between all parties concerned.

EARLY INTERVENTION

The ideal approach, of course, is early detection. The reasonable way to detect dyslexia is by relying on your personal observation, along with taking a thorough look at family history. This *does not* mean that every child with a family history of dyslexia is predestined to be dyslexic. In fact, for every dyslexic child in a family, there seems to be a gifted sibling who succeeds in getting his fair share of attention. Or you could have a gifted dyslexic child. Good luck!

BOOKS OF INTEREST

Fowler, Mary Cahill. *Maybe You Know My Kid: A Parent's Guide to Identifying, Understanding, and Helping the Child with Attention-Deficit Hyperactivity Disorder.* New York: Birch Lane, 1993.

Miles, T. R. *Dyslexia: The Pattern of Difficulties.* Springfield: C. C. Thomas Publishing Co., 1983.

Details the author's experience in assessing over 250 dyslexic children and young adults over a 20-year period.

School, Beverly, Ph.D. and Arlene Cooper, Ph.D. *The IEP Primer and the Individualized Program,* rev. ed. Novato, CA: Academic Therapy Publications, 1992.

Includes sample IEPs, a useful list of do's and don'ts, innumerable tips, and helpful checklists. Address changes mandated by the Individuals with Disabilities Education Act (IDEA). Order from: Academic Therapy Publications, 20 Commercial Boulevard, Novato, CA 94949.

Shepherd, Lorrie A. *Assessment of Learning Disabilities,* ERIC/TM Report 84. Washington: DC, ERIC Clearinghouse on Tests, Measurement, Evaluation, Educational Testing Service, 1982. Order from: Assessment and Evaluation, The Catholic University of America, 210 O'Boyle Hall, Washington, DC 20064-4035.

Rosenthal, Joseph H., M.D., Ph.D. *What To Do Until... The Learning Disabilitologist Arrives....* Oakland: Kaiser Permanente, 1994.

Learning disabilities, learning difference, or learning styles? Video presentation of ways to recognize, assess, and manage. Referral and prevention. Educational, psychological, and medical aspects. Order from: Department of Pediatrics, Kaiser Permanente Medical Center, 280 W. MacArthur Boulevard, Oakland, CA 94611.

5 TALKING WITH YOUR CHILD ABOUT DYSLEXIA

First, make sure the child understands he is not to blame for his learning problems. Calmly explain that dyslexia is not an incurable disease, but a manageable aspect of life. Point out the successes of other dyslexics as is seen in the many famous people who have managed to overcome dyslexia's challenges and used it to benefit their life's work. (See the list of famous dyslexics in the appendices.)

Second, let him know he is not alone. Share the statistics and explain that at least three of his classmates most likely have the same problem. They just aren't lucky enough to have been discovered.

Third, use the *D* word—dyslexia. Teach your child to do the same. Life is much easier when we don't have to keep secrets about who or what we are.

Finally, assure your child he has your unconditional love and support. Let him know he is lovable and special just because he's who he is. Say "I love you" often. Nothing fosters confidence and a good sense of self more than knowing we are held in respect and esteem.

DISCUSSING THE TEST RESULTS AND THE IEP

Keep the explanation simple. You don't have to go score by score, test by test. Such detailed information is more valuable to the examiner and the parent. What the child really wants to know is, "What's going to happen to me?"

Use the graph (page 42) to illustrate the deficit in written language as compared with other skill areas. Children understand graphs and accept their significance. Verbally go over the examiner's recommendations to acquaint the child with the kind of changes he may expect.

The IEP is the working blueprint for teachers and the guidance counselor, detailing the day-to-day curriculum. The IEP also instructs your child as to what will be different about his educational experience, what to ask for, and what to expect. The best way for your child to help himself is to learn how to ask for help before he is in trouble.

MAKING THE GRADE

If there is one valuable piece of advice for you to keep in mind, it is this: Do not take away privileges because of poor school performance. Punishing poor school performance for the dyslexic is like beating a dead horse. It amounts to nothing.

For some parents, nothing short of an A is acceptable. For others, C's and D's are considered normal and good enough. So that your expectations don't ride a roller coaster when it comes to grades, understand that dyslexics are notorious for inconsistency, earning an A one day and failing the next.

A Stanford University survey of 4,000 parents and 7,836 students shows that parents who are visibly upset by a child's grades only discourage better performance. According to Sanford M. Dornbusch, "The best way to exhort students to earn higher grades is to use low-key praise, encouragement, and offer to help."

Test pointers for parents to impress upon the child:
1. Child must get plenty of sleep; set routine bedtime.
2. Breakfast is a must; no skipping.
3. Cramming wears everybody out; stagger study periods.
4. Test anxiety is normal; use positive reinforcement.
5. Teach proper perspective; tests are not life and death matters.

THE PARENT'S ROLE: HOW MUCH HELP IS TOO MUCH?

I just finished tutoring Paige, an 11-year-old dyslexic student, who has poor organizational skills. She is highly motivated but lacks focus. She's been asked to create, organize, and then write, her science project. Her project was well researched but written in topsy turvy fashion on pieces of scratch paper with no common thread.

The key to helping Paige, and other students like her, is not to criticize or berate, but to ask them to envision their creation as a finished product, then backtrack to pull together the key ideas that led to the conclusion. The key ideas provide a skeletal outline for coordinating details collected on scratch paper. Your role as a parent is similar. Be supportive, not critical; lend a hand when needed; establish parameters or limits to your guidance. Here's a quick clue to how much is too much. If you are doing 50 percent or more of the work, you've been conned and are doing too much.

Often it is the mother who feels pressured to take over the teaching process for the child. Sometimes this works; other times it becomes a battleground. Your good intentions to teach reading, writing, or spelling to your child may end in frustration for the child and anger for you.

If you are so inclined, go for it. If not, help when you can, recognize your own limitations, and be willing to turn the actual teaching over to those outside the family. Don't waste one minute feeling guilty or thinking you have failed the child!

HOW TO CREATE THE ENVIRONMENT FOR SUCCESS

Support and encouragement from families are the primary motivators, beating out the influence of peers and teachers. There is a direct correlation between the role modeling of the parent and the motivation, doggedness, and determination of the child. This combination of toughing it out and persistence pays off in spades only when the child does his fair share, including making sacrifices.

This notion of sacrifice on the part of the dyslexic child may not sit well with you, especially if you consider the child handicapped and at a disadvantage from the start. Memories of your own difficulties in school may result in an overprotective relationship. Or perhaps, some unmet expectations may cause impatience or refusal to accept failure of any kind.

Let me help you resolve this issue quickly.

If the dyslexic child doesn't believe he has a vested interest in his academic success, then he will do as little as possible and you will be doing all the work. Understand that the dyslexic child has an inborn resilience and is well equipped with abilities to overcome obstacles. Capitalize on these abilities and you have a win-win situation.

THE PARENTS' CONTRIBUTION

Undoubtedly, the persons who most directly influence language development are the parents. You may be surprised to know that the dyslexic child learns more naturally by listening than by reading or trying to read. By talking to your child and reading aloud, you bring language into the free-flowing context of everyday use. This normal everyday flow of language helps the dyslexic understand the meanings of words, including the nuances of jokes and "meaningful" interpretation. Speaking and understanding speech is the way human beings communicate information, intelligence, and feelings. Therefore, language is more than just words.

It is equally important for dyslexic children to learn expressive (speaking) as well as receptive (listening) language skills. So, you be a good listener, too. Remember, language works both ways!

The dinner hour is a good chance for everyone to speak and be listened to. Because language includes listening skills as well as speaking skills, dinner presents a golden opportunity for everyone, including the dyslexic, who tends to be impulsive and interrupt, to practice language skills in a safe setting.

As parents, you can model good speech habits, and help your children use correct words and phrases. The dyslexic can learn to curb his impulsiveness, fine-tune good listening skills as well as proper speaking skills, and be part of the big picture, rather than left out.

WHAT ABOUT THE REST OF THE KIDS?

The dyslexic thrives in a home environment that teaches a spirit of cooperation, including problem solving and shared interests. The dyslexic should not be exempt from normal household rules. Everyone in the family should have a household responsibility, at least one chore that must be done on time, for these responsibilities are just more training for the real world.

One way to involve the dyslexic with each member of the family is to share interests and hobbies, games, and puzzles. You can also give the dyslexic a leadership role when it comes to choosing family outings (i.e., visits to the museum, zoos, historical sites, sporting and special events). Let him plan the outing from start to finish, then exchange the role with a family member for the next outing. Television is not all bad, and can be yet another shared interest to consider. Actually, proper exposure to programming can be great fun for the family and a fine way to utilize the best show-and-tell medium available.

If this sounds like a lot of work, it is. Again, the greatest impact on how a child learns is the home environment...every bit as important as the quality of the teachers or curriculum.

SOME POINTERS

- Be sure the dyslexic child understands his role in relation to the rest of the family. Spell out your role along with those of brothers, sisters, and significant others.
- Don't demand perfection. Discuss weaknesses and strengths, and decide how to balance.
- Do provide opportunities to participate in areas of special interests and skills outside the academic arena.
- Let the child know his identity does not hinge on success versus failure.
- Develop a daily program with the child, designating homework schedule, break time, reward, and extracurricular activity.
- For dyslexics, structure during the school week is best. More flexibility on weekends may be allowed.
- Help set realistic, not pie-in-the-sky, goals. Work up to the big one. Better to have a building block of small, defined successes to cushion the setbacks. This is how you help your child develop self-confidence.

WHAT ABOUT HOMEWORK?

Now this is the tricky part. My favorite place to study was the dining room table. Probably the reason I enjoyed that spot was because it was cleared after dinner. My own room was such a mess, I couldn't find a flat, unobstructed surface. Besides, the notion of a special study area never entered my mind...nor my mother's.

Also, I remember that the dining room was like Grand Central Station—the hub of family activity. Because I have good organizational skills, and the ability to concentrate in the midst of mayhem, the commotion did not interfere with my learning. On the other hand, my dyslexic grandson, Chris, gets easily caught up with the slightest distraction and immediately loses focus.

Because the dyslexic is easily distracted, he must have a quiet place to study, a desk or table at which to work, and books, especially a large-print dictionary and other reference materials at hand. Proper lighting is important. A good desk lamp and/or overhead lighting enhances the ability to focus and reduces eye strain.

A regular study time helps with the structure needs of the dyslexic. Blaring televisions, drop-in visitors, or telephone interruptions are out. The whole idea is to create an atmosphere of priorities for the student, with the understanding that there is a time for play and a time for work.

"Love comes first, but consistency comes second." So says Alan Ravitz, child psychologist, and other specialists who believe that children really want homework guidelines. This means designating specific hours after school for homework. A parent unwilling to step in with consistent rules will probably add to their child's academic anguish. Parental consistency, not parental toughness, is the most important homework aid.

Psychiatrist Bennett Leventhal echoes this idea and makes these suggestions for parents:

- Invite the student to designate their own homework hours. This issue, once decided is largely non-negotiable.
- Try to be home during homework hours.
- Encourage five-minute breaks after 20 to 40 minutes of honest homework.
- Harness television exposure. That stuporous look they get *is* actually a stupor.
- Establish a quiet hour every night.
- Check homework, especially with younger children. Let them know it's okay to make mistakes.
- Music? As long as they produce and you can stand it, don't worry.

WHAT IS NEGOTIABLE?

1. Homework hours.
2. Time out, especially when frustrated.
3. Completion of project ahead of schedule deserves reward. (Do not replace with more schoolwork!)

WHAT IS NON-NEGOTIABLE?

1. Homework hours, once decided, are non-negotiable.
2. Schoolwork comes before play or T.V.
3. Skipping homework.
4. Not turning in assignments.
5. Behavior in classroom.
6. Courtesy towards teacher.

This last point bears repeating.

If you are angry with your child's teacher, *keep it to yourself.* Then make a phone call to set up an appointment to discuss your concern. If your child is angry with his teacher, let him spout off, then decide whether or not to intervene.

The best way to help your child is to give him specific tips on how to handle the problem. According to psychologists John Clabby and Maurice Elias, strategies for problem-solving are based on three ideas:

1. Children's capacity to make thoughtful decisions is related to their capacity to cope with everyday problems.
2. These skills can be taught.
3. Adults who come in contact with children most often are in the best position to teach children these skills.

This means YOU, the parent, can help your child to:

• Articulate the problem
• Decide on a goal
• Check the consequences
• Plan, act, and rethink

You can rehearse the problem situation by assuming the role of teacher and allowing your child to practice his response. Follow up by more of the same. The best thing that happens is this becomes a good exercise for teaching the child how to deal with the day-to-day snags at school and his personal friendships. The worst thing that happens is it doesn't work.

If the problem is outrageous, like a teacher who repeatedly

humiliates your child in front of peers or, God forbid, slaps your child, boxes his ears, or pulls his hair, then you must spring into action and confront the teacher. It is a fact that children with learning differences, especially dyslexia, are frustrating to have in a classroom. But that's no excuse for abuse.

A Mother's Story

A mother in Oklahoma called NDRC one day in early September 1990. She was in tears; her story was deeply upsetting.

"My son, Jason, is 16 and in the eighth grade," she began. "He's been diagnosed as dyslexic and failed just about everything.... The principal concocted a plan to punish Jason for his failure by placing him in solitary confinement.

Every day Jason goes to school and sits in a room smaller than a closet, with no windows. His teachers give him his work, and naturally he doesn't do it. The principal believes this is a contest of wills and is determined to prove a point. I think the whole thing is crazy. I'm worried about my son. Can you help?"

First of all, I couldn't believe my ears. Second, I couldn't believe a parent would go along with such a ridiculous idea. I gathered my wits and told the parent, "Get your son out of that school immediately!"

Needless to say, the extremes some educators go to in order to experiment with failure are scary. In the course of my conversation with the mother, I asked if the school had her permission to carry out their "experiment." She said that they did, even though it went against her better judgment.

I spoke with the mother at length, outlining a game plan to help her son. When we finished talking, she said she felt much better knowing there were real options for her son, one of which happened to be a private school in nearby Tulsa, Oklahoma, which specialized in dyslexia remediation.

The mother called back about a month later to give me an update. She had contacted the Oklahoma Education Agency to voice her complaint; also, she received literature from the Oklahoma Client Assistant Program. The upshot of the dilemma was placement of Jason in the private school in Tulsa; he was eligible for financial aid, which provided a one-year scholarship.

The blessing in this case was the option. Most parents don't have that option and are forced to deal with the existing school system. Again, arm yourself with the resources and information available, and demand that your child's school provide services.

If they refuse, you know what to do.

TELEVISION IS NOT THE BOOGEYMAN

Today, television is under fire for excesses in violence, sex, and profanity. Parents are concerned, with good reason, over the explicit moral decay of programming aimed at young audiences. The situation is frustrating for parents wanting to do the right thing, and for producers who need to respond to market demand.

Taken at its best, television *can* be a powerful educational force in children's lives. The Action for Children's Television (ACT) organization offers these suggestions to help children gain the most benefit from television.

1. *Talk about television with your children.*
  • Talk about differences between make-believe and real life.
  • Talk about violence and how it hurts.
  • Talk about programs that delight or upset them.

2. *Look at television with your children.*
  • Look out for television behavior that children might imitate.
  • Look for television characters who care about others.
  • Look for television characters who are competent and praiseworthy.

3. *Choose television programs with your children.*
  • Choose the number of programs children may watch.
  • Choose to turn off the set when the program is over.
  • Choose to turn on educational programs.

Because multisensory techniques, audiovisual in particular, are vital to the learning process for dyslexics, television and the VCR can be considered godsends. Television documentaries, such as those shown on PBS or the Discovery Channel are fabulous examples covering science, geography, culture, humanities, history, and the like. Many literary classics have been made into movie classics, and can be rented from the library or video stores.

Also, creative individuals associated with television are quite candid about their personal battles with dyslexia. Steven Cannell, writer/producer for *The A-Team* and *The Rockford Files*; Harry Anderson, the judge in *Night Court*; Henry Winkler, The Fonze from *Happy Days*, now in a new series, *Monty*; Brook Theiss, who plays Wendy Lubbock on the sitcom, *Just the Ten of Us*; and Tracey Gold from *Growing Pains*, are just a few of the many talented dyslexics who have made a name for themselves in show biz.

WHAT ABOUT COMPUTERS

Computers are another electronic godsend for dyslexics. Research shows the computer hooks the right-brain functioning of the user, which is the creative-thinking skills area. Dyslexics are creative thinkers, therefore, most dyslexics take to computers like fish to water.

According to Peter McWilliams, author of *Personal Computers and the Disabled*, the computer has three superhuman qualities: infinite patience; inexhaustible energy; unlimited availability. Let me address each quality as it relates to dyslexia.

1. Patience—The computer is nonjudgmental and never gets angry. What this means is that the computer will present the same math problem a thousand times, if that's what it takes for the student to get the answer.

2. Energy—It doesn't matter if it is 10 A.M. or 8 P.M., when the computer is turned on, it's ready to go.

3. Availability—To be used or not used, it is up to the student's personal desire. The next lesson is available when the student is ready, not when the teacher is available.

The beauty of the word processing function of computers boils down to one simple fact: it reduces the mechanical burden of writing by allowing for editing, moving blocks of text, and inserting omissions (which is the bane of dyslexics!). It is so easy to make changes that it encourages rather than discourages careful editing of work for spelling, grammar, punctuation, and style.

The printed text aids dyslexics with spelling because print physically matches our visual image of the word in memory. Additionally, the print factor is a huge equalizer for those with indecipherable handwriting. The ability to delete, move, and spell check is the icing on the cake, totally eliminating the need to erase and recopy entire writing projects.

In a nutshell, computers are limited only by accessibility to the types of software available for the dyslexic. Special software for students and special education software are available from the Cambridge Development Laboratory, which represents more than

100 publishers of software compatible for Apple, Macintosh, and IBM.
For catalog information, contact:
Cambridge Development Laboratory, Inc.
86 West Street
Waltham, MA 02154
1-800-637-0047

FRUSTRATION OR HOW TO KEEP YOUR COOL

It's easy for me to tell you to remain calm, cool, and collected when dealing with your dyslexic child. It's next to impossible to be anywhere near rational when you find a month's worth of homework crumpled and tossed under his bed. Your heart pumps wildly and you see red.

For starters, take a deep breath.

Next, take another deep breath. Please do exhale this time, and count to 10 (or 100 if you need to).

What is really going on at this moment (in psychological jargon) is transference. Your reaction reflects the dyslexic's frustration with his own deficiency. Believe it or not, dyslexics are perfectionists. When they hide or destroy their work, it's because they're already convinced it is not good enough. Rather than chance being criticized, they'll do away with completed assignments even though the work contains no errors.

Seriously, the best advice for dealing with frustration is, *take care of yourself first*. Compare your situation to boarding a plane with a child. The flight attendant instructs you to put the oxygen mask over your face first, then tend to the child; to do otherwise places both you and the child in jeopardy. Use that illustration to navigate those inevitable exchanges of frustration between you and your dyslexic child.

Train your dyslexic child to do the same and you both benefit. Misplaced frustration goes nowhere. Frustration, pointed in the right direction, can soften anger and create trust. Give it a try!

A SENSE OF HUMOR HELPS

Here's my Golden Rule for the parents of dyslexic children. Use humor to deflect utterly ridiculous situations. Apply the rule not only to children, but to grownups, too.

Humor is a remarkable tonic for whatever ails us. Mixing

laughter with the serious business of home, work, and school is essential to maintain a healthy family. Everyone feels better after a good belly laugh!

In *Human Development*, Diane Papalia and Sally Olds explain the relationship of humor to language. "…jokes are told for the sheer joy of showing mastery over language, using mispronunciations and wrong words, making puns, telling riddles, telling stories that depend for their humor on basic knowledge or on different meanings of a word, so children can show off what they know…."

Jokes are the "in" thing for elementary school kids and a rite of passage for socialization. The gift of laughter serves as a release for anger, frustration, and helps minimize anxiety. Buy your dyslexic child a joke book with large block print, and let him practice telling you jokes from the book. Explain the joke if he doesn't get it. After a while, he'll memorize favorite lines and enjoy trading jokes with friends and family alike.

The Golden Rule has a postscript that reads as follows:

1. Never tease a child.

2. Never ridicule a child.

3. Never make a child the butt of a joke.

4. Never, *never*, make fun of a child's mistakes.

GREAT WORDS FROM A GREAT MAN

DON'T ACCEPT ANYONE'S VERDICT THAT YOU ARE

LAZY, STUPID, OR RETARDED

by

Nelson Rockefeller

(In response to "The Puzzle Children," broadcast on PBS, Fall, 1986.)

"…I was one of the 'puzzle children' myself—a dyslexic or 'reverse reader'—and I still have a hard time reading today.

"But after coping with this problem for more than 60 years, I have a message of encouragement for children with learning disabilities—and their parents.

"Based on my own experience, my message to dyslexic children is this:

- Don't accept anyone's verdict that you are lazy, stupid, or retarded. You may very well be smarter than most other children your age.

- Just remember that Woodrow Wilson, Albert Einstein, and Leonardo da Vinci also had a tough problem with their reading.
- You can learn to cope with your problems and turn you so-called disability into a positive advantage.
- Accept the fact that you have a problem—don't try to hide it.
- Refuse to feel sorry for yourself.
- Face the challenge.
- Work harder and learn mental discipline—the capacity for total concentration.
- Never quit.

"If it helps a dyslexic child to know I went through the same thing....

But can conduct press conferences today in three languages...

And can read a speech on television...

(Though I may have to rehearse it six times)...

With my script in large type...

(And my sentences broken into segments like these)...

(And long words broken into syllables)...

And learned to read and communicate well enough to be elected governor of New York four times...

And to win congressional confirmation as vice president of the United States..."

BOOKS OF INTEREST

Bloom, Jill. *Help Me to Help My Child*. Boston: Little, Brown, 1990.

Includes guidance and resources necessary to cope with obstacles both in and out of the classroom. A step-by-step plan of action to ensure the child has the best education possible as well as a renewed sense of self-esteem.

Clark, Louise. *Can't Read, Can't Write, Can't Talk Too Good Either.* Baltimore: Penguin, 1974.

In this intensely tender book, the author (mother of a dyslexic child) presents a personal account of a family's struggles with dyslexia.

Fleming, Elizabeth. *Believe the Heart: Our Dyslexic Days.* Falls Church, VA: L.F. Publishing, 1984.

A personal account of one family—a mother and her five children, all of them hereditary dyslexics—told in straightfoward terms. Order from: L.F. Publishing, P.O. Box 3175, Falls Church, VA 22042.

Holley, Shelby. *A Practical Parent's Handbook on Teaching Children with Learning Disabilities.* Springfield: Charles C. Thomas, 1994.

Gives parents a guide to help design and implement an effective remedial program. Shows how to make realistic changes in the physical and emotional environment at home and at school.

MacCracken, Mary. *Turnabout Children: Overcoming Dyslexia and Other Learning Disabilities.* New York: NAL-Dutton, 1987.

Explains ways in which the author, a therapist, has helped learning-disabled children in their lives at home and at school.

McWilliams, Peter A. *Personal Computers and the Disabled.* New York: Quantum Press, 1984.

Describes ways in which disabled persons can use computers. Explains how software and hardware can be adapted to suit particular needs.

Osman, Betty B. *Learning Disabilities: A Family Affair.* New York: Warner, 1989.

Suggests ways in which learning-disabled children can be helped both in school and at home. Emphasizes the role family members play in guiding these youngsters toward higher levels of learning and independence.

6 WORKING WITH YOUR CHILD'S SCHOOL

When the National Commission on Excellence in Education published *A Nation at Risk* in 1983, they hit the nail on the head. Public education in the United States was decaying faster than rotted wood. The fallout from this decay became a national disgrace, measured in statistics like the existence of 90 million functional illiterates in the U.S.

When I refer to one who's functionally illiterate, I mean a person who cannot fill out a job application; cannot read anything beyond the daily newspaper (most written between sixth- and eighth-grade reading levels); and/or cannot keep or advance in a job because of poor reading skills.

William J. Bennett, then U.S. Secretary of Education, responded to the commission's report in 1988 by encouraging us to "become a nation of readers." Dr. Bennett advanced the idea that "education begins in the home and flourishes when it draws upon the combined efforts of children, parents, teachers and administrators." And, I agree totally.

Now, having said that, I want to bring you closer to the heartbeat of a public education system that historically fostered literacy, but has become a springboard for social experiment and is quickly slipping through our fingers.

64

Schools are basically made up of wonderful, hard-working, dedicated teachers like my daughter-in-law, Lisa. Lisa works from dawn until dusk, and sometimes on the weekends. There are thousands like her out there; teachers who love teaching and want to help children succeed.

Then, what's wrong with our schools and how did it happen? It happened the day parents turned the upbringing of their children over to the school. Aided and abetted by "social reformers," every issue imaginable was unloaded on schools under the guise of public education. Every issue, that is, except The Three Rs.

What this means is that teachers like Lisa, who are supposed to teach academics, spend the major part of their day (and all of their energy) on social problems. And guess what? Lisa's in-service teacher training is not on subject matter. It is on discipline in the classroom.

Where do you, as a parent, and where does your dyslexic child, as a student, fit in the overall education scheme? To begin, pretend that you and your child are players on a "wheelie" team. The rest of the team includes the superintendent, school principal, teachers, counselors, coaches, and others. Each player has an important position on individual spokes of the wheel, which is perfectly balanced and ready to roll.

What I've just described is an example of the finely tuned relationship between parent, student, and school. However, the balance of the moving wheel depends on the cooperation of all the players. If one team member suddenly gets off the wheel, unannounced, the wheel becomes wobbly. If two or more jump off at the same time, the wheel becomes seriously out of balance. If only a few of the players remain on board, the wheel finally falls over.

The dyslexic student can't do it alone and be successful in the classroom. Teamwork is the key. And remember, you are not *just* a parent. You are a major player on the team.

PARENT INVOLVEMENT

Traditionally, parents have been excluded from the educational process. The standard commitment to excellence in education is determined by linking professional partnerships (educators) with their ideological goals. The partnership goals are worthy and well intended. But conspicuous by its absence is the goal that needs to be first on the list.

"The missing education goal is parent involvement," says Pat Henry, past president of the National Parent Teacher Association. In June 1991, the National PTA formally targeted comprehensive parent-involvement programs in every U.S. school as a priority. The goal is definitely worthy and well intentioned, but unfortunately, still the best kept secret in town.

I call it unfortunate because more often than not, the only contact between parent and school occurs under adversarial conditions, with enough blame to go around, 10 times over. Raymond Wlodkowski and Judith Jaynes explain that this adversarial relationship is the result of "no prior contact...no opportunity to build mutual trust...." And it only gets worse.

So, how do you avoid blame and approach the school?

BRIDGING THE GAP

Approach the school with the objective of establishing teamwork firmly fixed in your mind. YOU orchestrate the relationship between your dyslexic child and the school. Remember, it's not how brilliant you are in presenting the facts, but rather, how tenacious you are in maintaining the link.

START WITH THE TEACHER

I know how busy you are, but by investing a small amount of time at the beginning, you can pave the path to better communication between you, your dyslexic child, and his teacher, with better results in the long run.

You can do this by simply:

1. Organizing thoughts, concerns, and helpful ideas about your dyslexic child on paper.
2. Contacting the teacher by phone or in writing to open communication.
3. Offering assistance in the classroom or after hours (i.e., volunteering for teacher's aid, room mother, consultant, phone committee).
4. Sharing information about your family that will alert the teacher to extenuating circumstances (i.e., divorce, illness, job loss, new baby, relocation, etc).
5. Helping out with field trips, class parties, and projects.
6. Reinforcing the teacher's helpful suggestions concerning your child's schoolwork, homework, and conduct.

Get Involved with the School

The best way to know the school personnel and for them to know you is by getting involved. How can you do this?

1. **VOLUNTEER.** Sign up for a committee that allows you to showcase your special skills. You don't have to chair a committee, just join the group and have fun.
2. **ATTEND.** Show up for school events. Be a familiar face at PTA meetings, science fairs, fall/spring open houses, and fund-raising efforts.
3. **SUPPORT.** Stand up for extracurricular school programs. Many after-school programs (i.e., sports, choir, band, clubs, etc.) benefit your child's social, physical, and creative needs.

Learn "Who's Who" in School Administration

Do you know the name of your school district's superintendent? The president of the school board? The school counselor? How about the principal and the assistant principal? You probably know the person who answers the phone at your child's school. If so, that's good! Messages between home and school generally cross the school secretary's desk first. The secretary can direct you to the proper resource, thus saving you wasted phone calls and frustration.

Make every effort to familiarize yourself with the staff at your child's school and the district administration office. Most schools publish a directory with such information. Believe it or not, name recognition goes a long way toward resolving a small problem that could mushroom into a major fiasco.

How the Dyslexic Fools Everybody

No teacher wants to see a student fail. Moreover, no teacher wants *their* student to fail. Therefore, a symbiotic relationship exists from the very beginning. The student is there to learn and the teacher is there to teach. Sounds good on paper but here's the reality, and a phenomenon well known to dyslexia experts.

The dyslexic fools everyone, even teachers, with his ability to perform in the classroom *in spite of non-existent basic reading skills.* Just ask any adult dyslexic how he faked his way through school and you will be amazed at his story. Here are just a few:

"...the teacher called on Neil [to read], and the kid next to him began feeding him words in a whisper, and the kid on the other side did the same. You know people who have learning disabilities learn to fake. And Neil really had learned to fake."—Barbara Bush, talking about her son Neil's struggle with dyslexia

◆ ◆ ◆

"...In my early school years when large pictures accompanied schoolbook texts, I was called 'brilliant' by my teachers. Later, when my reading started to slow down, I was afraid of losing my title, so I manipulated it. I did everything but tell people I had trouble reading."—Harry Anderson of *Night Court*

◆ ◆ ◆

"...I was...the chubby little kid who was the stupidest kid in class...I survived by cheating and daydreaming..."—David Dean, head of Landmark School's drama department, Boston

◆ ◆ ◆

"...I was surely the dumbest kid in school....I memorized my music for the sax and pretended to be playing from sheet music..."—Malcolm Alexander, sculptor and artist, Ft. Worth, Texas

◆ ◆ ◆

Dyslexics are great pretenders. That's how they survive. But inside, they hurt...a lot. So don't you be fooled either.

HOW TO GET COOPERATION

Now that you understand the dyslexic's modus operandi and you are a familiar face on campus, get ready to go to work! Remember, you know your child better than anyone else. Besides, you are also armed with an IEP and/or written plan for accommodation.

Getting the accommodation is one thing. Getting the school

to implement it is another. Potential problems can be nipped in the bud if you:

1. Make sure the IEP lists every service your child needs, including frequency and amount of time it will be offered.
2. Visit with each of your child's teachers at the beginning of the school year. Give teachers a copy of the IEP.
3. Leave a telephone number where you can be reached during the day if a problem arises.
4. Assure the teacher(s) of your willingness to cooperate.
5. Follow through with recommendations made by the teacher(s) concerning your child's study habits.
6. Initiate conversations with the teacher(s) when in doubt.
7. Check daily with your child to stay on top of his progress (or lack of progress).
8. Teach your child to ask for help.
9. Clearly identify problems; separate fact from hearsay.
10. Use informal solutions whenever possible (much less costly in terms of time, money, and resolution).
11. Use assertiveness in expressing concerns.

WHAT WORKS FOR DYSLEXIC STUDENTS

I'll bet you were wondering when I'd ever get to this part. The "cure" for dyslexia has been debated forever, so my suggestions are based on the consensus of educators who work with dyslexic children and adults on a daily basis. The results are so-so with some, and breathtaking with others. The wide variation of results can be attributed to:

1. The fact that some children are more severely dyslexic than others.
2. The method of remediation is faulty.
3. The duration of remediation is too short.
4. The child doesn't want to cooperate.
5. The school doesn't want to cooperate.
6. The parent denies the problem.

Let's talk about all of the above in relation to what works best for the dyslexic child.

VARIATIONS IN DYSLEXIA

"Dyslexia," according to Dr. Sally Shaywitz, "is...like hypertension, occurring along a continuum with graduations and degrees. Children who test 'mildly' dyslexic one year may test 'normal' the next and not get the help they need."

When a child is tested early, like in first grade, the I.Q. and achievement point spread is generally wide if the child is dyslexic. As the child continues in school and is tested again, the point spread shrinks. This happens because poor reading ability undermines not only verbal skills, but also word problems in math, science, social studies, etc. The general overall performance is affected, causing a decline in point spread, which on paper means the child is no longer dyslexic and therefore not entitled to services from the school. Remember, early detection establishes a baseline for future testing.

Let me describe a worst-case scenario. By third grade the undetected dyslexic is already two years behind; by fifth grade he is fighting for his life (and maybe repeating a grade); by eighth grade his self-esteem is destroyed and he gives up; by tenth grade he is a high school dropout.

However, because you have taken all the right steps and are well informed, you understand the degree of severity as it pertains to dyslexia. You also know how the dyslexic fools everyone, including his teachers. As a result, you refuse to have remedial training for your dyslexic child put off any longer.

No teacher available to provide dyslexia remediation in your child's school? Not to worry. Tell the school principal that you have a list of teacher-training resources designed for dyslexia remediation. The resource list is included in the appendices.

REMEDIAL METHODS THAT WORK

Remediation means retraining. The dyslexic student must be taught in a different way because he didn't learn in the first go-round. The buzzwords for dyslexia remediation are: **individualized, phonetic, multisensory, structured, sequential**. Some of the better-known methods are Orton Gillingham, Slingerland, Alphabetic Phonics, and the Herman Method. The methods listed are not, by any means, the only ones available. You can check out the credibility of a remedial method by making sure it incorporates these factors:

    1. Individualized. A reading program tailored to the dyslexic student's ability level and learning style.

2. **Multisensory.** Presenting information in a way the student can see it, hear it, and feel it.
3. **Intensive Phonics.** Synthetic phonics requires the student to learn letter sounds first, then blend to create words. Analytic phonics can then be used to take the student to the next step, which is to use what they know about letters by sight, add consonants, and form a new word.
4. **Meaning based.** Writing is an excellent way to tap a student's understanding of language. One cannot compose with words one does not understand.
5. **Systematic. Structured. Sequential.** Student builds on what he knows. New material is not presented until he has mastered the basics.
6. **One on one or small groups.** The student-teacher ratio is small. Either one on one or small group (no more than three).

So what else is new? The method described makes perfect sense. Isn't that how my child is taught now? No! Your child participates in a system that uses the "look-say" method, which is also called the "whole-word" method. The whole-word technique uses a simple concept whereby the student is shown the word with a corresponding picture. For example, displayed next to the word "boat" would be a picture of a sailboat. Most students memorize the whole word and recognize it later. Not the dyslexic. The dyslexic memorizes the *picture* and the corresponding word's sound. Take away the picture and the dyslexic doesn't have a clue as to what the word is. So he makes a wild guess. Because he cannot synthesize words, he guesses and says, "ship" (because he remembers the picture). "Ship" and "boat" don't look anything alike, but are close enough in meaning to carry the dyslexic through that moment, until the terrifying next moment when he has to spell the word in a spelling test.

MORE REMEDIAL TECHNIQUES: MODIFICATION

Lest you think modification techniques are mollycoddling, consider the alternative. According to Priscilla Vail, author of *Smart Kids with School Problems*, adaptations made in the school curriculum take varying learning styles into account and give more students the chance to succeed. The dyslexic student is a case in point, with strengths in one area masked by weakness in another.

Modification techniques include:

- Student takes regular exam with extra time given.
- Student has access to tape-recorded textbooks.
- Student can tape record classroom lectures.
- Teacher gives oral exam to student, who responds orally.
- Peer tutoring: another student assists with class material.
- Notetaker: another student shares class notes.
- Tutorials: student meets with teacher before or after school.
- Content mastery: teacher reviews regular classroom material.
- Learning center: teacher helps with homework assignments.
- Classwork modification: teacher uses multisensory techniques.
- Homework modification: assignment is limited to key ideas.
- Study skills: student learns how to organize schoolwork.

HOW LONG WILL YOUR CHILD BE DYSLEXIC?

Once dyslexic, always dyslexic. Impress this fact upon the school system responsible for your child's education. Public schools in the United States uses a rule of thumb for ongoing remedial services—not by the special education manuals, you understand, but in reality. The reality is this: once a student tests normal, special services end. The school offers to reinstate services only if the student is failing. Then you, the parent, get to start the special-accommodation process all over.

Avoid wasting precious time with your dyslexic child's education by refusing to allow the suspension of services. Do not agree with any proposal to wait until your child fails before resuming services. A sure-fire way to keep the remedial process in place is to coordinate the necessary phases of your dyslexic child's education up until high school graduation. You can do this by reviewing your child's IEP at the end of each school year. Make sure all services are in place for the following fall semester before you sign the IEP.

A QUICK REVIEW

- **Phase I**—Remedial reading, writing, and spelling classes are provided for the dyslexic student (one on one or small group).
- **Phase 2**—Modifications in the regular classroom are established. (See the modification techniques listed on previous page.)

• **Phase 3**—Orientation to the IEP and "what works" is supplied (by you!) to each of your child's teachers.

WHAT IF MY CHILD IS ANGRY AND REFUSES TO COOPERATE?

Luleen S. Anderson, Ph.D. advocates telling the child how you feel and asking for consideration. "Help the child understand the causes of stressful situations," she adds. "Children can begin to react properly once they understand the reasons for their frustration." Be straightfoward about what the remedial plan calls for and why. And don't over-react with tough rules, regulations, and punishment

According to Dr. Anderson, bad discipline involves punishment that is unduly harsh and inappropriate, and it is often associated with verbal ridicule and attacks on the child's integrity. Good discipline includes creating an atmosphere of quiet firmness, clarity, and conscientiousness, while using reasoning. This approach helps children develop respect for themselves and others.

WHAT IF THE SCHOOL REFUSES TO COOPERATE?

Generally speaking, the school is inclined to be cooperative. There are exceptions to the rule, however, and that is why you will have this book in hand when confronting the recalcitrant principal. Arm yourself with the facts and you can't go wrong. However, if after exhausting all avenues, the school refuses to have your child evaluated, remediated, or accommodated, you do have recourse.

Every state department of education has an appeals process, whereby an impartial hearing officer looks at the facts and makes an independent legal decision. Usually, this takes 30 days, and 15 days more to implement.

If a satisfactory conclusion is not reached, you then can file a civil lawsuit in state or federal court. Check your (state) Client Assistance manual for details.

THE PARENT DENIES THE CHILD IS DYSLEXIC

What parent would refuse to help a child who is having trouble with learning? No loving parent would think of doing such a thing. Right? Wrong! There are parents who believe the child should tough it out "just like they did." Denial is rooted in fear, anger, and shame. A doctor may not want to admit his only son is a "C" student. A CEO may hide the fact that his daughter is in the "dummy" class (special education). Or, parents may ignore school recommendations because they, too, have problems with reading, writing, and spelling, and cannot help their children academically.

If you are undecided, ask yourself: Is it in my child's best interest to fall further and further behind in school, or is it in his best interest to be as successful as possible? Let common sense be your guide.

THE TEENAGE DYSLEXIC

Melvin D. Levine, pediatrician and director of the Division of Disorders of Development and Learning at the University of North Carolina, describes the adolescent dilemma: "In high school it is critical to be able to recall in April what you learned in October." Dr. Levine goes on to explain the continuum of dyslexia, adding "Some students have trouble with long-term memory. Some…with language difficulties have trouble expressing themselves… and live in mortal fear of being called upon in class …Another big problem is automatic memory…it is exceedingly difficult to think and write at the same time."

Compounding the dilemma is the fact that the close partnership between the dyslexic student, parent, and school now shifts. Some parents are reluctant to let go of the teenage dyslexic. At the same time, the dyslexic teen is straining at the bit, ready to move away from his comfortable environment and take on new challenges.

The moment of truth, when all your hard work pays off, is high school. By now, the dyslexic student has a pretty good idea of his learning style and what works best for him. It is time for a role change.

A STRATEGY FOR HIGH SCHOOL

"When your teenager enters high school, begin teaching the self-advocacy role," recommends Margaret Dietz Meyer, Ph.D., an advisor for learning-disabled students at Ithaca College in New York. Until now, you have been the dyslexic's advocate. High school is the perfect time to start transferring this role to the student. Here are some tips to help this process along:

1. The student is included in parent-teacher conferences, ARD committee meetings, and IEP planning.
2. The student assumes ownership of learning goals, as well as responsibility for day-to-day decision making.

3. The right to disclose information about his dyslexia belongs to the student.

4. The student centers on his abilities (strengths).

The dyslexic high school student is just like every other teen. He has a million distractions to deal with, not the least of which is his daily struggle with Algebra, Chemistry, Spanish, and those god-awful English compositions. He must juggle abilities as well as disabilities, but what he wants most is empowerment.

The key to empowerment for the dyslexic teenager is self-advocacy. It's up to you, the parent, to pass the baton. When he accepts, give yourself a pat on the back for teaching him so well. Parents can support the student in his new role by:

1. Discussing and outlining strategies.

2. Monitoring results.

3. Helping him re-group if the strategy doesn't work.

4. Encouraging follow-through by student.

5. Stressing abilities versus disabilities.

Now that you have successfully balanced the relationship between student and school, let's check out community resources and extracurricular activities for your dyslexic child. Social skills are not the dyslexic's best asset; therefore, activities to help him nourish self-esteem and develop friendships are important considerations. Low-cost or no-cost programs exist in every neighborhood. And the best part is, these programs are tailored for your child's special needs.

Books of Interest

Cronin, Eileen. *Helping Your Dyslexic Child.* Roseville, CA: Prima Publishing, 1993.

A step-by-step program for helping your child improve reading, writing, spelling, comprehension, and self-esteem. Covers psychological aspects of managing the dyslexic child along with vocabulary and syllable rules.

Johnson, Barbara, EdD. *Helping Your Child Achieve in School.* Novato, CA: Academic Therapy Publications, 1985.

Offers readers a number of ways to support and help preschool as well as middle-grade children succeed by developing comprehension and reading skills through a series of simple at-home educational activities. Order from:

Academic Therapy Publications, 20 Commercial Boulevard, Novato, CA 94949-6191.

Levine, Mel, M.D. *Keeping A Head in School.* Cambridge, MA: Educators Publishing Service, Inc., 1991.

A book for students about learning disabilities and learning disorders. Helps students understand their strengths and weaknesses as well as to appreciate their individuality. Also available on cassette. Order from: Educators Publishing Service, Inc., 31 Smith Place, Cambridge, MA 02138-1000.

Smith, Sally. *No Easy Answers.* New York: Bantam, 1993.

Describes clearly what the learning-disabled child is like. Gives the best advice available on how to live with him and how to teach him.

U.S. Department of Education. *What Works.* 1986.

Research about teaching and learning. Published by the U.S. Department of Education. For a free copy write to: Information Office, OERI, 555 New Jersey Avenue, NW, Room 300, Washington, DC 20208 or call 1-800-424-1616.

Van Reusen, A.K Ph.D., C.S. Bos, J.B. Schumaker, & D.D. Deshler. *The Education Planning Strategy.* 1994.

A motivation strategy manual for parents and students. Demonstrates preparation methods for conference and techniques for communicating effectively during a conference. Order from: Edge Enterprises, Inc., P.O. Box 1304, Lawrence, KS 66044.

Wlodkowski, Raymond J. and Judith H. Jaynes. *Eager to Learn.* San Francisco: Jossey–Bass Publishers, 1990

Discusses ways parents and teachers can work together to achieve shared goals of motivating their children and students.

7 WHAT YOUR COMMUNITY MAY OFFER

HOW LIBRARIES NURTURE LITERACY

Dyslexics get claustrophobic when surrounded by shelves of books. Not because they don't want to read (they desperately do!), but because they can't. The strongest library recollection for many adult dyslexics is that of bolting for the door out of cold fear or just plain embarrassment.

Are you one of those dyslexics who hasn't set foot inside a library in years? Or would your dyslexic child rather have the chicken pox than go to the library? Take heart. I have good news for all of you. Libraries of the nineties have become user friendly!

In October 1990, I served as a delegate to the Texas Conference on Libraries and Information Services. Making the role of community libraries relevant to new demands of the Information Age was a hot topic. In the end, we agreed that libraries, as uniquely equipped educational institutions, were in a perfect position to help promote the concept of family literacy.

Libraries are not simply places to encourage reading for

pleasure. Libraries play a fundamental role in educating the public through Learn-To-Read programs. Accordingly, libraries serve as major providers of adult literacy classes and sponsors of reading activities targeted for preschoolers up to senior citizens.

It is predicted that by the year 2000, 71 percent of the labor force in industrialized countries will work in the information and communications sectors of the economy. For that reason, Information Age families need access to a centralized, multimedia resource. Where is the most logical place to centralize books, periodicals, online databases, archives, and other records? The public library. How does the dyslexic child or adult fit into the grand scheme of the Information Age? How can the library help him succeed?

Today's librarians are tuned in to the needs of non-reading adults. They also are trained to recognize and assist children with reading difficulties or dyslexia. Librarians love books; they want to help dyslexics learn to love books, too.

Librarians can help dyslexics with the following print aids, which are essential tools of the Information Age.

1. Large-print books
2. Books on audio cassette
3. Video cassette movies
4. Voice-synthesized reading machines
5. Computerized search programs
6. The Talking Books Program

LARGE PRINT BOOKS

Large-print books are available to the general reading public. Ask the librarian to orient you to the children's large-print book section, and the adult large-print books as well. Just about everything imaginable, including best-sellers, modern novels, and classics, are available in large print.

BOOKS RECORDED ON CASSETTES

Much of what is available in print is also available on audio cassette. Libraries openly display audio-recorded books for general public use. A regular two-track machine will play the audio book cassettes.

VIDEO CASSETTES

Classic and popular movies are on loan at your library. These are great aids to accompany your dyslexic child's reading material. (Think multisensory!) Vocational overviews, career updates, and special interest topics are some of the choices included in the video library selection.

VOICE-SYNTHESIZED READING MACHINES

Reading machines or voice-synthesized text readers, such as the Kurzweil Reading Machine, are small computers with an optical scanner that converts printed words into synthesized speech. Check to see if a reading machine is in place at your library, or if you are a college student, at your academic library.

COMPUTERIZED SEARCH PROGRAMS

Computerized search programs are fantastic resources for dyslexic students seeking information about a specific topic. For the dyslexic who is familiar with computers, the search is quick and simple. In many cases, a reference librarian will do the search for you. Some of the more common on-line search programs at libraries are:

ERIC—Clearinghouse of educational references

INFOTRAC—Periodical index; health references

EPSCO—Newspaper, magazine, periodical full texts

WESTLAW—Legal information; Supreme Court decisions

AUTOGRAPHICS—Government documents

CASSIS—Tracks patents, trademarks

In particular, you need to familiarize yourself with the ERIC (Educational Resources Information Center) network. ERIC is a centralized database clearinghouse of educational references on topics such as disabilities and gifted education, adult career and vocational education, and assessments and evaluations. ERIC also has a document reproduction service and can access just about anything in print that pertains to education (for a per-page fee). Some public and university libraries permit users to search ERIC CD-ROM databases free of charge.

In addition to using your local library as a resource for accessing ERIC's materials, you can contact ERIC on your own for additional information on specific topics. The contacts listed below are a couple of the network members available:

Disabilities and Gifted Children
Council for Exceptional Children
1920 Association Drive
Reston, VA 22091-1589
(702) 264-9474
1-800-328-0272

ACCESS ERIC
Aspen Systems Corporation
1600 Research Boulevard
Rockville, MD 20850-3172
(301) 251-5506
1-800-LET-ERIC (538-3742)

Other library CD-ROM search directories contain material listed under these directory names: The Library of Congress, Facts on File, Inc., National Genealogical Search, Art Index, Daily Newspapers, and Import-Export Data.

Usually there is a small charge for the information search or print-out. Again, in most cases the librarian does the search for you.

TALKING BOOKS AND OTHER TALKING-PRINT AIDS

When we think about dyslexia, we think of a hidden disability. It would seem that everything about dyslexia is "hidden," including resources available at a low cost or at no cost. Another fine resource is the Talking Book Program.

To meet the special needs of patrons who have learning disabilities like dyslexia, libraries are affiliated with the National Talking Books Service of the Library of Congress. A four-track playback machine is required for the Talking Books, and is free upon request for eligible persons. To obtain eligibility requirements for audio-recorded services, and a catalog of titles, contact your state library. (See the appendices for listing of state libraries.)

Local Talking Book agencies are staffed by volunteers trained to read assigned books that are recorded on cassette. Print-handicapped individuals (dyslexics) can request local recording services to record specific works if the state library does not have the requested material converted to cassette. The local reading agency will consider textbooks for dyslexic students from kindergarten through college, as well as work-related and other printed materials. Materials to be read must be supplied by the individual making the request. Usually, it takes six weeks to record a specially requested cassette.

The cassettes produced locally are standard two-track and can be played on any cassette player. A library of master tapes is developed so that many textbooks are readily available. The dyslexic child, college student, and adult are perfect candidates for the Talking Books program. Each local reading agency has eligibility requirements and there is a small charge for the cassette tape. A list of local volunteer agencies is available from your state library or you may contact:

National Library Services for the Blind and
Physically Handicapped
Library of Congress
1291 Taylor Street, NW
Washington, DC 20542
1-800-424-8567
(202) 707-5100

Talking Books are not a crutch! Nobody thinks twice about using a calculator as a convenient, quick way to get an answer to math problems. A Talking Book is simply the "calculator" of words.

Although the library provides literary reading material on tape, and local recording services are available, you need to know about an organization in the private sector that specializes in providing student textbooks on tape. It is a nonprofit organization called Recording for the Blind, Inc.

RECORDING FOR THE BLIND, INC.

Another great program is Recording for the Blind, Inc. (RFB), which provides taped textbooks and professional materials on loan to persons who are dyslexic or learning disabled. To participate, an application must be completed and signed by an appropriate professional. Eligibility criteria is flexible, but there is a small registration fee. BookManager is an information retrieval software package available to registered RFB borrowers. Information categories available from RFB's bookshop for use with BookManager include computer science, general reference books, psychology, finance, law, and classic fiction. You can contact the national office for information, along with a catalog of materials offered on tape at:

Recording for the Blind, Inc.
20 Roszel Road
Princeton, NJ 08540
(609) 452-0606
1-800-221-4792 (for orders)

Each of the recording services, the Talking Books programs of the National Library Services and Recording for the Blind, Inc., have extensive catalog listings of books available for the dyslexic, in large print or on cassette tape. Remember the distinction between the types of books provided. Talking books are primarily literary general-interest titles (including best-sellers, westerns, histories, biographies, self-help books) and recorded magazines. Recording for the Blind offers educational and professional books in all subjects and at all academic levels from fourth grade through postgraduate studies.

OTHER RESOURCES AVAILABLE IN THE PRIVATE SECTOR

Many educational materials for special-needs students (dyslexics) are created by teachers and available from publishing companies. Some of the companies that specialize in designing classroom teachers' aids include Lakeshore Curriculum Materials, Co., DLM Teaching Resources, Barnell Loft, LTD, and Curriculum Associates, Inc. In general, the materials are for professional use, but parents can order catalogs. Check with your library for a listing of publishers.

There are literally hundreds of teaching aids available for dyslexics. These aids are mainly categorized as compensatory or remedial. Compensatory aids subsidize or counterbalance the lack of skills in a specified learning area. Remedial aids re-teach using detailed, structured, and sequential formats designed for repetition.

Computerized compensatory and remedial programs are among the fastest growing teaching aids available. Schools, libraries, and universities already access these tools. You can access them, too. Let's take a look at some of the more popular devices.

VOICE SYNTHESIZED COMPUTERS—COMPENSATORY PROGRAMS

Desktop optical scanners that are more portable include Reading AdvantEdge and BookWise. The scanner recommended for dyslexics is BookWise (or BookWise/Edge), which is a PC-based tutoring system that scans books, converts the text into synthesized speech, and actually reads aloud to the student.

As material is read, it is highlighted by word, phrase, or sentence to help with visual tracking. The reader chooses the reading speed, voice, screen color, and print preference. Unique features include: syllabification, spell check, dictionary access. The reading machine is attached to a PC (286 or above) and operates by automatic scanner.

BookWise is compensatory (aid), *not* remedial (retrain).

Voice-synthesized reading computers are presently in use in schools, libraries, and community colleges. For more information, contact:

Xerox Imaging Systems, Inc.
9 Centennial Drive
Peabody, MA 01960
1-800-248-6550

TECHNOLOGY TODAY

Other resources that have voice-synthesized/voice-activated/large-print systems include Apple Computer Disability Solutions (1-800-600-7808) and IBM Special Needs Programs (1-800-426-4832).

TALKING AND LISTENING COMPUTERS— COMPENSATORY PROGRAMS

Microcomputer-based learning systems that talk to the user are not unusual, but are you familiar with computers that listen? One of the tools of tomorrow is a unique computer that recognizes voice patterns and converts speech to text on a computer screen (DragonDictate).

Another program uses synthesized speech to improve the reader's decoding skills by pronouncing the word or the word segments when highlighted with the computer's mouse (DECtalk).

Both programs are designed to serve as self-contained, teacher-independent systems with large built-in vocabularies for voice recognition (speech to text) or voice output (text to speech).Contact these companies for additional information:

DragonDictate DECtalk
Dragon Systems Digital Equipment Corp.
320 Nevada Street 146 Main Street
Newton, MA 02160 Maynard, MA 01754-2571
1-800-825-5897 1-800-344-4825

CASSETTE BOOKS OF INTEREST

Many of the books of interest (listed at the end of each chapter) are available on cassette. Cassette versions of print material are routinely produced by today's publishing companies in response to public demand for such aids.When you go to a bookstore or to the library, ask if the book you want is on cassette.

TALKING CALCULATOR

Eight-digit LDC display will add, subtract, divide, multiply, and calculate percentages. Four different speeds for hearing the answer. Available in English and Spanish from Independent Living Aids, Inc., 27 East Mall, Plainview, NY 11803, 1-800-537-2118.

EXTRACURRICULAR ACTIVITIES

Doesn't the dyslexic have enough worries without the burden of one more thing to do? You are so right. The dyslexic has worries, indeed. However, the dyslexic has one worry he can't escape, no matter how hard he tries. He desperately wants to succeed at something, and worries incessantly that he'll succeed at nothing.

Since the academic arena is a daily battleground for the dyslexic, other ways to master achievement become necessary. Extracurricular activities are a natural consideration, so let's examine first things first, from the dyslexic's point of view. Social skills are not the dyslexic's best trait. He knows this better than anyone else. In part, this stems from lack of self-confidence. Another part is inherent behavior attributed to the dyslexic's self-absorption. You've heard the jibes: airhead, space cadet, goofball, retard. Dyslexics internalize these names, believing they *are* what they hear. The second consideration is the dyslexic's clumsiness. He trips over his own feet, bumps into the crystal display at the department store, and weaves a path of destruction by his mere presence.

Extracurricular activities can be the perfect solution to help the dyslexic conquer low self-esteem, rise above ridicule, and overcome his clumsiness. Extracurricular means everything under the sun, from sports to music to art to hobbies and the like. The best way to introduce your dyslexic child to what's out there is take him to watch the activity. Then talk to him about his likes and dislikes, strengths and weaknesses, in relation to his participation.

The key to making the right choice when it comes to extracurricular activities is to encourage your child to select the activity *he desires*. More often than not, parents make the choice, based on their own love of the activity. The child is reluctant to argue, because he doesn't want to let the parent down.

The end result is not a pretty sight—better to have a happy, energetic child, because that's what counts. Stress causes worry, and heaven knows, the dyslexic doesn't need any more worries.

TEAM VERSUS INDIVIDUAL SPORTS

Because you want your dyslexic child to be part of the group, the first activity you opt for is a team sport. The YMCA, City Parks and Recreation, Boys Club, and Girls Club are great places to sign up for such activities. Not only do team sports teach individual skills, but the spirit of cooperation is highly contagious for the rest of the participants. Everyone, from parent to coach to score keeper, feels good and is part of the team. If your dyslexic child is gregarious and outgoing, team sports are a natural.

What if your child is not a team player? No problem. Every skill that is taught in team sports is the same in individual sports. If he is shy and withdrawn, he may not opt for the chummy, back-slapping, rough-and-tumble sport. This is not to say he will never play team sports. Individual sports can be a way to build self-confidence in preparation for team sports, if the dyslexic so chooses.

Look at it this way! Any sports activity is better than none at all. Individual sports usually become wonderful lifetime activities. Or, your dyslexic child could even become a world-class athlete and Olympian, like Greg Louganis or Bruce Jenner, who reached the pinnacle of success in spite of their difficulties with dyslexia.

POINTERS FOR PARENTS OF ATHLETES

1. Enthusiasm: make sure child loves what he is doing.
2. Balance: keep everything in perspective.

3. Winning: do not demand a child win.
4. Losing: do not blame or demean if he loses.
5. Decisions: the child must take part in decision making.
6. Abilities versus disabilities: teach the child that strengths and weaknesses go hand in hand.

CHECK OUT THE COACH

Coaches are important teachers as well as role models. The majority of community-sponsored sports programs recruit volunteer coaches who are certified in first-aid and CPR. It won't hurt to ask if your child's coach is a member of the National Youth Sports Coaches Association or the American Coaching Effectiveness Program.

Stick around during practice sessions. This is a good way to see the coaching staff in action with your dyslexic child. Here's a checklist you can use to quickly determine whether the coach is the proper mentor for your dyslexic child.

1. Does the coach ignore or interact with your child?
2. Does the coach give complicated directions or too many directions too quickly? Better to have the dyslexic work in smaller groups until the rules of the game or order of play is understood.
3. Telling is not enough. Does the coach also demonstrate? Dyslexics learn better by imitating the coach or instructor.
4. Is the coach patient or does he make derogatory remarks? Directional games like soccer or basketball can confuse the dyslexic; sometimes they forget which goal they are going for. Good coaching solves this problem quickly.
5. Does the coach have a win-at-all-cost attitude or is he truly interested in the socialization and fun aspect of children's sports? It's easy to check this out. Just listen to what he says *after* the game.
6. Does your child like his coach? This is the make-or-break point. There's nothing worse than being miserable when you're supposed to be having fun.

Your role as parent is the same as always. Remember, you are your dyslexic child's advocate. Therefore, your job is to ensure your child's safety, well-being, and opportunity for success. The rest is up to the coaching staff, and the athlete himself.

SPORTS OVERVIEW

Swimming—Enjoyable competitive sport for dyslexics. Swimming lanes define the perimeters when there are directional deficits. Builds heart and lung strength and endurance and develops body composition.

Wrestling—A good individual competitive, contact sport (if you can stand watching your child being twisted like a pretzel). Good for strength and endurance. Lots of ribbons and trophies.

Football—High-impact sport; focuses on teamwork. Football plays are complicated. Encourage the child to consider a position with simple parameters, (i.e., center or nose guard). Good for strength and flexibility.

Baseball/Softball—A high-skill team sport with lots of individual input. Good for coordination and balance.

Track and Field—A fairly adept child can find a niche for developing talent. Good sport to develop endurance and power.

Tennis—A high-skill individual sport that is regimented and quite competitive. Good for hand–eye coordination and heart–lung workout.

Basketball—Great, widely available team sport. Can be played by just about anyone. Good coordination and heart–lung workout.

Volleyball—A fast-moving, highly enjoyable sport. Good for hand–eye coordination.

Soccer—Excellent sport for early age. Teaches skill, conditioning, and coordination.

Gymnastics—Excellent individual sport. Develops proficiency in balance and tumbling; builds strength and flexibility. Definitely good for coordination.

Ice-Hockey—Fast-paced, rough sport. Good for balance and coordination; heart–lung conditioning.

Skiing—Cross-country skiing builds muscles; involves skill and fitness. Good heart–lung workout.

Some dyslexics are gifted athletes who have talents far beyond the average person's abilities. If your dyslexic child has natural ability, then by all means, encourage him to go for the gold! If athletic ability is not his gift and causes him to worry, it is time to move on to greener pastures. There is something for everybody.

BOY SCOUTS OF AMERICA PROGRAMS

The Boy Scouts of America (BSA) has 330 local councils with groups divided into age and program level. BSA philosophy is geared toward non-competitive participation. The boy scout is encouraged to work at his own speed. Troop leaders are trained to recognize and appreciate individual differences.

The best way to get information about scouting, according to Conrad Fruehan, National Boy Scouts of America associate director, is to check the white pages listing in your local telephone book. BSA publishes a manual entitled *Scouting and the Learning Disabled* that includes good tips for parents and volunteers interested in scouting.

BOYS AND GIRLS CLUB OF AMERICA

The Boys and Girls Club of America (BAGCA) encourages mainstreaming of their participants, as well. BAGCA has a publication called *Mainstreaming Matters*, a guide for staff and volunteers who work with learning-disabled children. For further information, contact:

Boys and Girls Club of America
1230 W. Peachtree Street, NW
Atlanta, GA 30309
(404) 815-5700
1-800-854-2582 (for local referral)

OTHER SKILL-BUILDING PROGRAMS

Most national and international groups that serve children and youth have a policy of mainstreaming children with disabilities into regular programming. The professional staffs for the YMCA, the YWCA, Camp Fire Boys and Girls, and Girl Scouts in your community are attuned to the special needs of children and can recommend a program that just might be a perfect fit for your child. Check the white pages in your phone directory for the organization(s) nearest you.

SUMMER CAMPS

Summer camp is a great experience for dyslexic kids because it teaches them to function without parents and fosters independence. Summer camps usually focus on special-interest themes. This means your dyslexic child can attend a summer camp that includes academics as part of the activity, or strictly adheres to a single theme. Do your homework and check all this out in advance. Also, check to see if the camp is registered with the American Camping Association (ACA). ACA also has a placement service to help parents make the best selection.

Summer camps provide exciting competition for participants. Medals, ribbons, and certificates are great for self-esteem. To help with the decision-making process, consider the following:

Philosophy—Does it match yours? Make sure the camp's ideology follows your beliefs and the way you teach your child.

Location—Is it local? Out of state? Another country?

Background—How long has the camp been around? Most camps have a track record and references you can verify.

Programs—Is it suited to your child's needs? You need to think about why this particular camp is a good idea.

Facilities—Are they clean and well maintained? See camp in action beforehand.

Participants—Who comes to the camp? Is the camp co-ed or boys only/girls only? Groupings should be age-relevant.

Staff—Is there a good staff–participant ratio? Small groups are better for more individualized attention.

Cost—Does expense fit your budget?

Scholarship—Are scholarships available? Always ask.

MUSIC AND THE ARTS

Dyslexic children are auditory, visual, and kinesthetic. This means they respond to what they hear, what they see, and what they touch. This is also why we use the term "multisensory" (hear, see, touch) when discussing ways to teach dyslexics.

Written language is two dimensional. Music, art, dance, and drama are three-dimensional. Dyslexics function best in a three-dimensional world, which is why so many dyslexics are creative individuals. The arts are yet another way for the dyslexic to learn in a non-threatening, spontaneous environment.

Drama—Actors are forced to rely on their bodies, their voices, and one another.

Music—Uses auditory skills, building on natural ear for music. Helps acquire mathematical skills.

Dance—Balance, coordination, free spirit. Strength and stamina; can mimic personality by movement.

Creative Writing—Great for language skills. Utilizes imagination and technical know-how. Forces normal word order with a creative twist.

Visual Arts—Strength: recognizes patterns of shape, form, and color. Dyslexics usually have excellent visual memory. Leads to development of reading skills.

BOOKS OF INTEREST

American Camping Association. *American Camping Association's Guide to Accredited Camps.*

Lists over 2,000 camps and 400 retreats, coast to coast. Also indexes specialty camps. Call 1-800-428-CAMP to order annual guide.

Cooper, Ann McGee. *Building Brain Power.* Dallas: McGee-Cooper and Associates, 1982.

Presents key ideas of right-brain-left-brain functioning, with the viewpoint that 90 percent of brain potential is untouched. Discusses creativity, daydreaming, vocabulary development through right brain. Order from: P.O. Box 720368, Dallas, TX 75372, 1-800-477-8550.

Gree, Diana Huss. *Parents' Choice.* Kansas City: Andrews and McNeel, 1993.

A sourcebook of products to educate, inform, and entertain children.

Micheli, Lyle J. *Sportswise.* Boston: Houghton Mifflin, 1990.

Discusses what has changed in the way kids "play" today. Provides expert advice on solving fitness issues facing parents. Also gives tips on how to work with schools and coaches to create a safe program for your child.

Fetterolf, Michele, ed. *Peterson's Summer Opportunities for Kids and Teenagers.* Princeton, NJ: Peterson's Guides Inc., 1994.

Complete details on over 1,400 different summer programs offered by private schools, colleges, camps, travel and sports groups, and religious organizations.

8 What About College?

A fellow teacher recently told me that dyslexics never make it to college. I immediately enlightened my colleague, saying "Of course dyslexics go to college! Why not?" "But they can't read!" my colleague insisted. "Dyslexics are better suited for vocational school." Taken aback at the ignorant remark, I said, "Vocational schools require reading, too, so what makes you think dyslexics can't succeed in college as well?"

Needless to say, we had quite a discussion about dyslexics, college, and a whole series of other misconceptions about dyslexia.

The idea that dyslexics are resigned to careers that offer no challenges and require no academic background because they have trouble with words is pure myth. College *is* one of many logical steps for dyslexics after high school. Let me explain.

Any pursuit after high school amounts to a transition of some kind. Certainly, trade school, or vocational instruction, or any other honorable post-secondary training can figure into the equation. Whatever the dyslexic decides to do, it is his choice and rightfully so.

However, regardless of his career path, there is no occupation indexed under "skill only." The same prerequisites apply to every advanced schooling situation. Reading, writing, and math competency are standard criteria whether the dyslexic attends a two-year community college, four-year university, or a ten-month technical training school.

As a parent, you understand the progression of learning for the dyslexic better than anyone. You know that his achievement is constant but "delayed" with respect to academics, maturity, and self-image. Besides his developmental lag, you can't help but think about all the years of hard work, the modest successes and near failures. Bothersome memories of the past make you uneasy about the future, until you can no longer avoid the hard question: "Is my dyslexic child ready to make the proper transition from high school toward the real world?" Put your mind at ease…

You will be happy to learn that the variety of postsecondary options available to the dyslexic are limitless and include programs tailor-made for his interests, special needs, and growth potential. You can help lay the groundwork for the dyslexic's passage from high school to beyond by familiarizing him with:

1. The broad range of occupation and career opportunities.
2. Aptitude and interest assessments to determine objectives.
3. Work experience, either part time or summer employment.
4. College entrance requirements and testing dates.
5. Independent living experience (i.e., camp, retreat, or travel).

Are you wondering how you could possibly do this, how there could be enough hours in the day? Where do you begin? Start by contacting your dyslexic child's high school counselor. The counselor's job is to facilitate the transition from high school to college or the workplace. Furthermore, the counselor has access to all kinds of information about:

1. Postsecondary schools
2. Admissions testing schedules
3. Aptitude-interest assessments
4. Career-occupation inventories
5. Work/study programs

In the meantime, find out the dates of school-sponsored events such as:

1. College Night—Representatives from colleges and universities come to the school. This is the best opportunity to gather information and visit with an alumnus. The dyslexic student needs to attend when he's a sophomore or junior. Don't wait until senior year to check out potential schools.

2. Job Fairs—Source for summer jobs for teenagers. Local companies recruit on campus for temporary or part-time job opportunities.

3. SAT or ACT Prep Courses—Generally offered on Saturdays. Test-taking techniques offered; good for dyslexics who suffer from the jitters before, during, and after tests. (And most do!)

4. Mini-Courses—College majors presented in mini-segments so student can experience the field content.

5. Career Day—Professionals come to school and meet with students to discuss what they do on the job and why they chose that career. Usually broken down by professions: medical, legal, media, education, social work, public relations, interior design, etc.

6. Job Site Tours—Students visit the actual job site, meet with employees, and see the business in action.

7. Industry Visitation—Representatives from community industries come to school (similar to College Night). A good opportunity to get first-hand information, collect brochures, and check out industry as a prospect.

YES! There Are Real Options for Dyslexics

Throughout this chapter, I will give you pointers on how to access real options by using the system for the next level of the dyslexic student's education. Any institution receiving or benefiting from federal assistance (i.e., grants, student loans, capital improvement, etc.) must follow the guidelines outlined by Section 504 of the Rehabilitation Act of 1973. Because many post-secondary schools could not determine "reasonable accommodation" for dyslexic students, the Americans with Disabilities Act of 1990 helped clarify the issue for administrators, support personnel, and students.

The real options include:
1. Four-year college or university
2. Community college
3. Trade school
4. Vocational training
5. Supported employment internships

The College-University

The admissions process and prerequisites for college are basically the same for everyone. The dyslexic is not exempt from a level of performance that demonstrates ability to do the required coursework. What you need to remember is the **accommodation process** for admissions, which requires fulfilling eligibility requirements and paperwork, but can make the difference between being accepted or turned away. At the same time, investigate the programs and services offered by the school, making sure the program is not just on paper, but in fact, really does exist. The final, but equally important, aspect of the admissions process is to have college plan A, B, and C in place.

THE ADMISSIONS PROCESS, STEP BY STEP

Step 1: Admissions Requirements

The basic admissions requirements for most colleges and universities include the following:
1. High school diploma or GED certificate
2. SAT or ACT scores
3. Letters of recommendation
4. Personal interview

In addition, here's where your good record keeping during elementary and high school pays off. Documentation of dyslexia *before* college admissions is a definite advantage. The educational evaluations not only track the dyslexic student's scores over a long period of time, they are of immense value when it comes to acceptance and placement in special services programs.

Keep in mind, highly competitive schools are not out of reach for the dyslexic if he is qualified and can do the coursework. Remember, any school receiving federal money, including student loans, grant money, or disability scholarships must reasonably accommodate dyslexic students. The accommodations process for college admissions is your next step.

Step 2: Accommodations Process

First, let's talk about the GED, which is accepted by most colleges and universities in lieu of a high school diploma. The following outline describes accommodations available to dyslexic students. Eligibility requirements generally include a letter of request and documentation of disability.

GENERAL EDUCATIONAL DEVELOPMENT TESTING ACCOMMODATIONS

The administration of the General Educational Development (GED) Test adheres to a policy of fair testing standards. GED candidates with specific learning disabilities or dyslexia can apply for special accommodations in testing. The difficulty of the special editions of the test is the same as the print editions. However, the accommodations can include additional time, private testing, and frequent breaks. You can also request a reader, audio cassette version, or permission to use a calculator

You can get more information about the GED and other postsecondary education issues from the Higher Education and Adult Training for people with Handicaps (HEATH) by contacting:

HEATH Resource Center
One Dupont Circle, Suite 800
Washington, DC 20036-1193
1-800-544-3284

Other free single-copy publications you can get from HEATH include:
- "Getting Ready for College: Advising High School Students with Learning Disabilities"
- "College Freshmen with Disabilities"
- "How to Choose a College: Guide for the Student with a Disability"
- "Financial Aid for Students with Disabilities"
- "Vocational Rehabilitation Services—A Student Consumer's Guide"
- "Transition Resource Guide"
- "Education for Employment"

APTITUDE TEST ACCOMMODATIONS FOR COLLEGE

Dyslexic students may apply for special college entrance testing. Accommodations include untimed tests, tests on tape, or tests read by a tutor. Also, a computerized version of the GRE is now offered at designated testing locations. For additional information, contact:

ACT Special Testing
ACT Test Administration
P.O. Box 168
Iowa City, IA 52243
(319) 337-1332

Scholastic Aptitude Test (SAT)
Services for Students with
Disabilities
P.O. Box 6226
Princeton, NJ 08541-6226
(609) 771-7137

Educational Testing Service (ETS) offers special administration of college and graduate admission tests for dyslexic students. The SAT, GRE, and GMAT are offered in large print or on cassette. Other accommodations can include a reader, additional time and rest periods. For further information about ETS special services and eligibility requirements, contact: (609)921-9000.

Read the stipulations for college entrance examinations carefully. Preparation tools include study tapes, review courses, and mock tests. Usually the test is administered in a separate room to students with special needs. The student may also use a calculator during the math portion of the exam (SAT 1).

Step 3: Letters of Recommendation

Never underestimate the power of letters of recommendation. The letters can tip the scale in your dyslexic child's favor when it comes to acceptance by college admissions committees. The dyslexic student should solicit the letters from those who have made a difference in his life and truly believe in his ambitions, aptitude, and ability to succeed. The dyslexic will know who to ask when the time comes.

Step 4: The Interview

The personal interview is essential because, here, the cards are laid on the table. Now is the time for questions, answers, and honest appraisal. The interview may be the tie breaker if the dyslexic is wavering between this school or another.

During the interview, it is in the student's best interest to be honest about his dyslexia. He should come prepared with a list of questions about the types of accommodations and/or support services he will need for the next four or five years. Most interviewers are knowledgeable about the ADA requirements and readily provide the necessary information.

A personal interview can work in the dyslexic's favor if he presents himself well. One helpful strategy is to rehearse the interviewing process with a parent, counselor, or favorite teacher. The student's ability to self-advocate and be at ease with himself are major factors in a successful interview, and can be fostered through such role playing.

COLLEGE PROGRAMS AND SERVICES FOR DYSLEXICS

Never assume the special services program at the school of your choice is up and running. Always ask. These programs depend on funding and when the funding disappears, so does the program. Also, there is a difference between programs, services, and modifications.

Programs

A learning disability program offers a full range of support services and learning disability specialists. Staff should include at least one full-time specialist, two or more part-time support staff professionals, and auxiliary personnel to provide services. A program includes:

1. Learning lab with on-site support personnel
2. Remedial programs
3. Special skill development curriculum (math, reading, spelling, writing)
4. Specialized instruction and case-by-case services
5. Organization and study skill management strategies

Services

Specific on-campus service offerings for the dyslexic student should include, at minimum:

1. Diagnostic and prescriptive teaching services
2. Guidance and counseling services
3. Tutorial services

4. Vocational planning/job placement services
5. Learning-disability specialists
6. Advocacy services

Modifications

The word "modification" does not mean "less than." Modification is an adjustment to existing coursework that reflects the dyslexic student's achievement, not his impaired skills. Coursework modifications include:

• taped texts
• large-print text books
• note-taker
• tape recorder to tape class lectures
• untimed tests
• exams read aloud
• oral presentations instead of written exams

COLLEGE PLAN A, B, AND C

Barron's Profiles of American Colleges offers these suggestions when choosing a college that "will choose you."

Choice No. 1: The Most Desirable College

This is the Plan A dream school, the state university or private college your dyslexic child has talked about since day one. Even if entrance standards are a cut above his test scores or high school grades, other beneficial factors enter into the acceptance process (i.e., letters of recommendation, personal interview, parent is an alumnus, reputation of high school).

Choice No. 2: The Almost Most-Desirable College

This is the Plan B realistic choice, whose admissions requirements fairly meet your dyslexic child's capabilities and overall profile as a prospective student at the school. Although it's a good choice, there is still no guarantee of acceptance. However, keep in mind the beneficial factors I've listed can tip the process in your favor.

Choice No. 3: The Safety College

This is the Plan C "backup" choice, which could be a two-year community college or junior college. The third choice should not be regarded as an option that would be better than nothing. Keep this school in the running because it is a viable option, not simply the only option left. Many dyslexic students start at the community college, then move on to the four-year school they chose in Plan A or Plan B.

COMMUNITY COLLEGES

Today, hundreds of vocational and trade programs are offered through community colleges in coordination with the local business community. In addition, many community colleges have state-of-the-art programs, along with technical auxiliary aids, and services for dyslexics. Visit your community colleges and check out their programs since the quality and resources vary from campus to campus. Most have developmental classes for reading, writing, and math with supplemental support services.

Entrance requirements for community colleges are less stringent than those of their four-year counterparts. Nonetheless, basic standards, such as a high school diploma or GED, plus placement test requirements must be met. If the student lacks appropriate reading, writing, or math skills, he is referred to developmental classes to make up the deficit.

The same programs, services, and modifications discussed on pages 70-72 should be provided by the community college you are considering. As with a four-year program, always ask. Never assume. If the dyslexic student can substantiate his claim (again, here's where your record keeping pays off) it is a good idea to register with Disabled Services before the semester begins. Also, he should talk with his instructors and set priorities for coursework early. A great way to keep up with the current curriculum, as well as to preview future programs, is to get on the school catalog mailing list at least two years before the dyslexic student's high school graduation.

Besides providing a core curriculum for academic transfer to a four-year institution, community colleges have career training programs such as automotive technology, food management, real estate, etc. These are among hundreds of associate degree programs offered in partnership with corporations and local industry. Such programs usually have math, language, and/or science prerequisites.

A final word about community colleges. Most offer tele-courses and self-paced classes to accommodate the working student. Before signing up for any non-traditional class, the dyslexic needs to talk with a counselor and the instructor about course structure, content, and exam requirements.

Here's the bottom line for the dyslexic: Motivation is closely linked with performance. Students should not even consider enrolling in telecourses or self-paced classes unless they are highly motivated self-starters. Stick with the traditional course offering. It's a safer bet.

You can order the *Directory of Disability Support Services in Community Colleges* from the American Association of Community College Publications, P.O. Box 311, Annapolis Junction, MD 20701, (301) 490-8116.

MODEL SPECIAL SERVICES PROGRAM

There are scores of wonderful college special services programs in every state. When sorting out the school choice situation, how do you determine whether or not it is right? Simply pay attention to any red flags concerning attitude. The attitude of the college administrative staff, from admissions on, is a good indicator of the respect assigned to a school's special services program. Pride should be the key element. When schools love to brag about their special services center, you know the program is alive and well.

Because of the Americans with Disabilities Act, all public institutions must provide reasonable accommodations for dyslexics, at no charge. Private schools of higher education also offer support services. However, if the program is enhanced, usually there is an additional charge for services.

The three universities I mention below are examples of the many fine postsecondary schools with special-services programs. Why do I list these three? Because each each school uses a completely different approach in providing dyslexia-related programs and/or services, yet the success stories are similar.

THE JONES LEARNING CENTER

The **Jones Learning Center** at the University of the Ozarks, Clarksville, AR, serves as an enhanced support services program for learning-disabled and dyslexic students seeking a college degree. Students receive remedial instruction as well as specialized skills training according to their needs. The program is designed to work with dyslexic students one-on-one and on a small-group basis. Personal counseling is offered to help reinforce emotional adjustment, and compensatory aids are used for deficiencies in reading, writing, and spelling.

THE A.J. PAPPANIKOU CENTER ON SPECIAL EDUCATION AND REHABILITATION

The **Postsecondary Education Unit** at the A.J. Pappanikou Center, at the University of Connecticut, in Storrs, provides a support program for students with learning disabilities. The University Program for College Students with Learning Disabilities, the Technology Assistance Unit, and the Diagnostic and Prescriptive Service Unit are part of the Pappanikou Center services and programs. The center is a state resource in the area of developmental disabilities and shares research, remediation methods, and assessment techniques with other public and private institutions throughout Connecticut.

THE SERVICES FOR STUDENTS WITH DISABILITIES CENTER

Services for Students with Disabilities at the University of Nebraska, Lincoln (UNL), is a joint project under the coordinating sponsorship of the Affirmative Action Office and Student Affairs. The center works with each student on an individual basis, with emphasis on the student providing first-hand information about abilities, disabilities, and needs. UNL encourages flexibility and personal responsibility in professor-student relationships, with dual responsibility in problem-solving situations to encourage students' independence.

VOCATIONAL, TRADE, AND TECHNICAL SCHOOL

With the passage of the Americans with Disabilities Act of 1990, public schools of higher education were not the only postsecondary institutions affected. Trade, vocational, and technical schools also recognized the value of compliance. Many of the same accommodations for dyslexic students that are listed under programs, services, and modifications for college students are available in the private sector.

If an exam for licensure, certification, or diploma is required, you can request accommodations. Remember, check this out in advance so there are no surprises. One school's interpretation of reasonable accommodations may not match another's, nor your expectations as to what will be allowed.

You can contact the Accrediting Commission of Career Schools and Colleges of Technology to obtain a copy of the *Directory of Private Accredited Career Schools and Colleges of Technology.*

Director of Constituent Services
750 First Street, NE Suite 905
Washington, DC 20002-4242
(202) 336-6850

SUPPORTED EMPLOYMENT PROGRAMS

The Vocational Rehabilitation Commission (**VRC**) is a state/federal cooperative program that provides services to disabled clients, including individuals with learning disabilities such as dyslexia. An interagency transitional service exists between the Education Agency and the Vocational Rehabilitation Commission for each state.

What this means is, the dyslexic high school student may be eligible to become a client of the Vocational Rehabilitation Commission in his state. The Commission provides services to support the transition from schools or home to employment or supported employment. With supported employment, a job coach works side by side with the client to help with intensive job training and assist in job retention. VRC also helps with independent living services and transition to college or a vocational training program. To locate the Vocational Rehabilitation Commission office near you, see the appendices.

FINANCIAL AID FOR THE DYSLEXIC STUDENT

If, in fact, the dyslexic student is already a client of the state Vocational Rehabilitation Commission, he may be eligible for partial or full postsecondary tuition. Other financial aid resources include federal student aid for families at all income levels, low-interest loans, and cooperative-education programs (formal study/career-related work). There are many creative ways to finance an education for the dyslexic student, all of which require research and lots of paperwork. Keep copies of the forms you fill out to save time and prevent errors later. The information requested will need to be repeated each time you apply over the next four years. Octameron Associates offers these tips to help pay your way.

1. Apply for financial aid no matter what.
2. Submit financial-aid forms early.
3. Ask for help in filling out forms; a school financial aid officer can assist you. Accuracy is important.
4. Inquire about innovative tuition aid features (i.e., installment plans, matching scholarships, sibling scholarships, athletic scholarships, alumni discounts).
5. Special conditions, such as disabilities, can greatly increase student-aid eligibility. (Because increased funding is now available for states' "special programs," universities are anxious to spend present allocations so they can be eligible to solicit new funds for their programs.)

For their catalog titled College Money Guides, contact:
Octameron Associates, Inc.
1900 Mt. Vernon Avenue, Box 2748
Alexandria, VA 22301
(703) 838-5480

HOW THE DYSLEXIC PUTS HIS BEST FOOT FORWARD

1. Start the applications process at least one year before the planned enrollment date.
2. Visit as many campuses as possible. Include such visits during family vacations or visits to other states. It is never too early to start investigating possibilities.
3. When you have narrowed your choices to Plan A, B, and C, make appointments with admissions counselors for a personal fact-finding interview.
4. Be forthright with the admissions counselor concerning programs, services, and modifications you need.
5. Find out if there are extra charges for special programs.

CLASSROOM POINTERS

1. Sit toward the front of the classroom to minimize distractions and maximize eye contact with instructor.
2. Use a tape recorder during lectures; listen to the tape as soon as possible after class to refresh your memory.

3. Make note of any questions you have so they can be answered before exam time.

4. Plan on two hours of study time for each hour of class time. Figure this in when planning the semester and determining your course load.

5. Build in study breaks to avoid fatigue and overload.

6. Keep *one* calendar listing things to do with dates, assignments, appointments. Write these down; don't trust your memory.

7. Be prompt; learn to prioritize your time.

8. Keep appointments, or call ahead if you must cancel.

9. Stick to your plan; it will help you stay organized and on task.

10. Ask for help right away if you are having trouble.

LIVE AT HOME OR MOVE AWAY?

Most students want to live in a campus dorm. Some prefer an apartment close to campus. Others do not have a choice or make the conscious decision to live at home and commute to the nearby campus. Whatever the case, the decision to live at home or go away is important, far beyond economic consideration.

Letting go of dyslexic children is heart wrenching for many parents. They don't realize how tough it is until they actually face that moment when he prepares to leave. A large part of the reluctance in letting go is rooted in the daily monitoring of his academic growth, plus the fact that you have been his closest advocate.

Now he will be on his own. Can he make it without you? Yes! Now you can safely release your dyslexic child. It is time for him to become his own advocate. Because you have taught him well, not only will he survive, he will thrive.

BOOKS OF INTEREST

Lipkin, Midge. *The Schoolsearch Guide to Colleges with Programs and Services for Students with Learning Disabilities.* 1993.

Distinguishes between programs (staff, compensatory skills development) and services (tutoring, counseling) available at more than 600 colleges and universities. Very detailed information, summarized in chart form; includes L.D. contacts. Order from: Schoolsearch, 127 Marsh Street, Belmont, MA 02178.

Needle, Stacy, M.S., Ed. *The Other Route into College.* New York: Random House, 1991.

How to get into college when you can't depend on your grades or SAT/ACT scores; 235 alternative admissions programs.

Peterson's Guides. *Peterson's Guide to Colleges with Programs for Students with Learning Disablities.* 4th ed. Princeton, NJ: Peterson's Guides, Inc., 1994.

Most complete and accurate guide of its kind. Lists 1,600 two-year and four-year colleges offering special academic programs for students who need them.

Scheiber, Barbara and Jeanne Talpers. *Unlocking Potential: College and Other Choices for Learning Disabled People.* Bethesda, MD: Adler and Adler, 1987.

Teaches and assists reader throughout entire postsecondary process. Resource for considering, locating, and selecting postsecondary resources.

Straughn, Charles T. *Lovejoy's College Guide for the Learning Disabled.* New York: Simon and Schuster, 1993.

Up-to-date information on admission criteria, support services, academic character, degree offerings, and tuition costs.

9 WHEN THE DYSLEXIC CHILD GROWS UP

You know someone who is dyslexic. "Impossible," you say. "I don't know any dyslexics. Besides, how could I tell whether or not the person who sits next to me at work is dyslexic; the manager of my favorite restaurant is dyslexic; the well dressed, confident man walking into my company's corporate board room is dyslexic; the beautifully groomed, articulate chairwoman of the charity event is dyslexic?"

You can't tell. Remember, dyslexia is invisible. Then what does it matter? Why can't we just leave them alone? They didn't ask for our help, right?

It matters because these people *do* ask for help...in a roundabout way. If you are not familiar with the telltale clues, you will miss the plea for help. Mixed messages sent by the "hidden" dyslexic often lead to misunderstanding. Then, a rash judgment about the dyslexic is made by others, and hard feelings result.

This is not a call for pity. It is simply an explanation for puzzling behaviors you may have experienced with someone who is your co-worker, neighbor, shopkeeper. Maybe that someone is your brother, sister, cousin, or grandparent. Or, perhaps, that someone is you.

106

Today's adult dyslexic attended school before learning disabilities were recognized. He has struggled since childhood with his hidden handicap, which he is a master at covering up. The struggle is emotionally draining, yet he continues on, unaware that help is available. His greatest fear, that he will be found out, adds to his misery. Until that day when the pain becomes intolerable.

Those who finally do ask for help usually start with a psychologist or psychiatrist, hoping to unravel the puzzle that refuses to go away. Some find the answer. Others, not so fortunate, are more confused than ever. They eventually retreat behind safe, familiar defense mechanisms, and live silently with their shame.

The adult dyslexic is the dyslexic child, all grown up. Nothing is different, except now he pays a heavy price for his secrecy. The price is emotional pain that masks the real problem.

EMOTIONAL DISABILITY OR DYSLEXIA?

Misdiagnosis is the ultimate horror story adult dyslexics tell. The dyslexic goes into therapy because of problems with anger, frustration, distractibility, anxiety. The therapist hones in on the emotional turmoil and glosses over the fact that the person cannot read, write, or spell. Exhortations to "try harder" and "do better" only make the dyslexic feel worse. And he still can't read, write, or spell.

Many psychotherapists, like many teachers, do not have the formal training and knowledge to recognize learning disabilities. Compounding the issue, adults who suspect they may be dyslexic are convinced it's all their fault. They are ashamed to mention the fact they cannot read, write, or spell to anyone, not even their best friend. Besides, if they'd just tried harder....

THE FICTITIOUS ADULT DYSLEXIC

"He's a bright youngster. Don't worry. He'll outgrow it."

The adult dyslexic has heard that remark at least a million times. His teachers said so. His pediatrician said so. His counselor said so. Trouble is, dyslexics never outgrow it.

Dr. X, one of my graduate school instructors, advised a classroom of young teachers "not to worry about their dyslexic students since they'd outgrow dyslexia in a couple of years." I almost fell out of my chair when I heard his words. When I challenged

Dr. X's assumption, he advised me to drop his class and take it elsewhere! In truth, grown-up dyslexics hide their inability to read in many clever ways. Favorite one-liners used by adult dyslexics are:

"READ!!? Who reads nowadays? It's a waste of time."

"Never read a book in my life. Don't need to."

"I hate to read. It's boring! Besides, everything I need to know is on television."

"The words jump all over the page. It's my eyes."

"I get sick to my stomach when I have to read out loud."

"I forgot my reading glasses."

The most frustrating aspect about dyslexia is the fact that the burden of "proof" rests on the individual. Dyslexia is indeed an invisible disability, hard to prove or explain, but just as debilitating as other, more apparent, handicapping conditions. This is why early identification, evaluation, and remediation is so important.

Do you wonder where all these adult dyslexics are coming from? The fact is, they have always been present. Because dyslexia was not recognized, many hid their horror stories about school along with deep feelings of shame. Now it seems that more adults confront their own dyslexia when a family member or son or daughter is diagnosed. At this point they come to grips with their shame of the past, which continues to shade the present. Remember, when the dyslexic grows up, his dyslexia doesn't just suddenly go away.

Nolan Ryan, former power pitcher for the Texas Rangers describes growing up with undiagnosed dyslexia: "When I had that [dyslexia], they didn't diagnose it as that. It was frustrating and embarrassing....I didn't really know what kind of problems I had until I had kids. My boys both had it, and it was diagnosed early so they had special training, and both have overcome it quite well."

Many adults who come forward to speak about their dyslexia recall the painful memory of being called on to read out loud and failing miserably in front of snickering classmates. Even more humiliating is the fact that they are grown-ups now, with children of their own, and still have "trouble with words."

Not only do adult dyslexics continue to misspell, reverse, and omit words, they avoid reading out loud, afraid to risk reading even simple bedtime stories to their children or grandchildren. The problem is not psychological; it is dyslexia.

HOW TO RECOGNIZE ADULT DYSLEXIA

What if you are an adult and suspect you might be dyslexic? Or, perhaps you think a friend or co-worker may be dyslexic? The first step is to identify the individual by observing his behavior. Adults who exhibit the behaviors listed in the Adult Dyslexia Checklist are highly likely to have the hidden disability. Keep in mind, the checklist is not a diagnostic test. It is for identification purposes only.

ADULT DYSLEXIA CHECKLIST

- Reading, writing, spelling is markedly poor in contrast with average or superior skills in other areas.
- Avoids reading out loud. Omits or adds words when reading out loud. Reads very short passages, then quits.
- Complains of words "running off the page," "getting blurry," or "jumping around."
- Handwriting is poor, unusually large or childlike. Uses print lettering instead of cursive; has inconsistent slant; word space is uneven.
- Letter reversals: *b* for *d*; *p* for *q*; *teh* for *the*; *saw* for *was*.
- Directional confusion: up and down; right and left; in and out; back and front.
- Copying or note-taking is difficult. Written phone messages may have numbers reversed or out of sequence.
- Too many directions given at once cause confusion. Easily distracted; difficulty in paying attention; becomes flustered.
- Organizational skills are non-existent; loses things; repeatedly forgets appointments.
- Displays excessive anger, anxiety, or depression when cornered in a social or work situation requiring reading or writing.
- Misinterprets the nuances of language; doesn't get jokes; misses social cues.
- Describes school as a "nightmare." Problems have existed since childhood. Considered "trouble maker" or "class clown."

• Someone else in the family has identical behaviors/problems.

Other processing difficulties for the dyslexic can include:

Rigidity: Hates to change schedule; gets upset with unforeseen change in routine.

Impulsivity: Speaks or acts without thinking.

Perseveration: Dwells excessively on a point or repeats a joke beyond appropriateness.

Distractibility: Small noises, minor activity, or visual clutter cause loss of focus.

The dyslexic also has trouble:

At work: Needs a lot of supervision.
Makes careless mistakes.
Has difficulty organizing work or staying on task.

At home: Often doesn't seem to listen.
Fails to finish things.
Gets feelings hurt easily or is defensive.

At play: Clumsy or uncoordinated.
Misses social cues.
Tries hard but falls short.

IT'S NEVER TOO LATE

For the adult dyslexic, there is hope and help. You don't have to suffer in silence any longer. You can learn to read, write, and spell *and* manage your hidden handicap.

The good news: the right kind of help is available.

The even better news: it's available right where you live.

The best news of all: it's low-cost or free!

ADULT DYSLEXICS AND LITERACY

When 212 ABC stations and 313 PBS stations campaigned for Project Literacy U.S. on national television, literacy resources at the community level came alive. Some had been in place for years, but not truly appreciated or promoted as essential to the quality of the individual in the workplace. Now, a literacy hotline exists in almost every state. The hotline operator will refer the caller to the nearest community literacy provider(s).

A state-by-state listing of adult literacy resource centers with 800 numbers can be found in the appendices, or you can contact:
The National Literacy Hotline Contact Center, Inc.
P.O. Box 81826
Lincoln, NE 68510
1-800-228-8813
(402) 464-0602

Local adult literacy programs you may be referred to:
• Adult Basic Education (offered by the public school district)
• Literacy Volunteers of America
• Laubach Method
• Orton Gillingham Method *or* Slingerland Method
• Public Library Adult Literacy Programs
• Project READ
• PLUS Program
• Right-To-Read Program

The key questions you want to ask are:
1. What is the class size? (Small class size is better. There should be no more than 8 to 10 students per teacher.)
2. Who teaches the class? The instructor's credentials (i.e., a teacher's certificate and/or reading specialist training) are important, as well as experience working with adults.
3. Is the class remedial? What the adult dyslexic does not need is *more of the same.* (That's why they didn't learn in the first place.) The method *is* important. Refer to pages 70-72 and use the methodology outline as a guide.
4. How much will it cost? The instruction is generally free. You may have to purchase books and materials.
5. Where is the class held and at what time? Make sure the location and time is convenient; otherwise you will find excuses not to attend.

LITERACY IN THE WORKPLACE
According to the National Alliance of Business, it is estimated that by 1995, 14 million Americans will be unprepared for the jobs that are available. By the year 2000, the number of service-

producing jobs will increase approximately 25 percent, requiring higher-level skills. Those without basic skills will more than likely become unemployable.

The disappearing quality of our workforce is confirmed by statistics such as:

- Nearly 1 million youth drop out of school each year.
- 7 out of 10 high school students can't write a basic letter seeking employment or information.
- 3 out of 5 twenty-year-olds cannot add up their own lunch bill.
- 1 out of every 8 seventeen-year-olds is functionally illiterate
- 82 percent of all colleges and universities must now offer remedial training for students lacking basic skills.
- Michigan Bell reports that only 2 out of every 15 applicants for clerical positions can successfully complete the required written and typing tests.
- Motorola has found that 80 percent of its applicants cannot pass a simple seventh-grade comprehension or fifth-grade math test.
- At the New York Telephone Company, only 20 percent of those taking the operator's test (which measures reading skills) pass.

One innovative approach to forging a partnership between business and education is to identify and assist the dyslexic employee who is struggling to keep up with the fast-paced, changing demands of his job. He is a model employee with all the attributes corporate America desires. Not only is he honest and responsible, he helped the company through the lean years. Now he is in trouble. He needs help, but doesn't have a clue about what to do.

HOW TO IDENTIFY AND HELP THE DYSLEXIC EMPLOYEE

The possibility of a hidden handicap may account for the puzzling failures in model employees. Remember, the dyslexic employee is the dyslexic child all grown up. He continues to hide his disability behind the guise of forgetfulness or has a system in place whereby he manipulates his co-workers to cover his mistakes. Let me pose the question:

Do You Know This Employee?

- A model employee who is bright, motivated and dependable, but has puzzling failure in one area of his job
- A dependable employee who, when given a promotion, suddenly becomes unable to cope
- An earnest, hard-working employee who listens attentively to oral instructions, but then cannot remember them
- A verbally adept employee who spends much time trying to hide reading, spelling and writing difficulties

The employee usually is highly valued and a person the company wants to retain. However they have difficulty with:

- Receiving and processing information through their senses (eyes, ears, touch)
- Their brain telling their body what to do
- Selective attention, information processing, memory retention and retrieval, utilization of feedback and carrying out intentions
- Listening, talking, reading, writing, math or getting along with others

A workplace scenario could go like this:

QUESTION: How can the dyslexic employee be helped?

ANSWER: First, he must be identified, then approached.

QUESTION: What if he denies the problem?

ANSWER: He won't. But he might quit rather than address the problem.

QUESTION: Why would he do that?

ANSWER: Because past failures with learning to read, write, and spell are too shameful to repeat. He thinks it is hopeless.

QUESTION: How do I convince him otherwise?

ANSWER: Tell him you have a literacy in the workplace program or will allow him to attend a community literacy program on company time.

QUESTION: He's afraid "everyone" will find out he can't read.

ANSWER: Everyone already knows. Furthermore, everyone will be relieved the truth is out.

MODEL IN-HOUSE EMPLOYEE LITERACY PROGRAMS

Some companies have found in-house literacy programs to be cost effective and successful. Other companies have fledgling literacy programs, but don't want to advertise the fact they have employees who cannot read, write, and spell. Either way, the problem of functional illiteracy remains, and corporate America is left to deal with the issue sooner or later.

Companies like Hewlett Packard, General Motors, Eastman Kodak, Tandy, Scott Paper Company, and General Dynamics already address employees' needs with successful in-house literacy programs. If you, or someone you know at work, cannot read, write, or spell, ask your employee assistance person about a literacy in the workplace program. Even small businesses are cooperating with literacy efforts to help improve employee productivity.

THE AMERICANS WITH DISABILITIES ACT(ADA) AND THE DYSLEXIC EMPLOYEE

As described in chapter 3, the ADA basically states: "Employment discrimination is prohibited against qualified individuals with disabilities." Hence, the ADA protects individuals with disabilities, including those who are dyslexic.

Employment provisions of ADA apply to private employers, state and local governments, employment agencies, and labor unions. As of July 26, 1994, employers with 15 or more employees are covered by title I (employment provisions) of the ADA.

A condensed version of what the ADA says about the relationship between employer and the dyslexic employee is best defined by answers to these questions:
1. What is employment discrimination?
2. Who is a qualified individual with a disability?
3. What is reasonable accommodation?
4. How does the ADA protect dyslexics?
5. What are some of the modifications recommended for dyslexics?

EMPLOYMENT DISCRIMINATION

Employment discrimination is job bias in relation to the hiring, firing, advancement, compensation, training, and other terms, conditions, and privileges of employment. Persons discriminated against because they have a disability are protected under the terms of the ADA. Qualified applicants with a disability, including dyslexics, have a right to equal employment opportunity.

A QUALIFIED INDIVIDUAL WITH A DISABILITY

A qualified individual with a disability is a person who can perform the "essential functions" of the position with or without reasonable accommodation. A person with a specific learning disability or dyslexia will not be considered unqualified simply because of an inability to perform marginal or incidental job functions. The dyslexic can "self-identify" and request reasonable accommodations, but the employer must observe section 503 requirements of the Rehabilitation Act of 1973 regarding the manner in which such information is handled. The employer cannot use it as grounds for refusing employment unless it is job related and consistent with business necessity.

REASONABLE ACCOMMODATION

The employer is not required to make reasonable accommodation if it would impose "undue hardship" in relation to the size, resources, and structure of the employer's operation. With that in mind, the dyslexic can suggest reasonable accommodations and negotiate the action with the employer. Most accommodations can be handled case by case, with the employer acting in good faith. If agreement cannot be reached without intervention, complaints can be filed with the Equal Employment Opportunity Commission (EEOC).

PROTECTION FOR DYSLEXICS

Dyslexics are protected by the ADA as "qualified individuals with a disability." The impairment must substantially limit one or more major life activity, such as learning, working, seeing, or speaking. The dyslexic has a right to request modifications if he wishes to do so.

MODIFICATIONS THE DYSLEXIC MAY REQUEST

If the dyslexic expects accommodations or modifications, it is the individual's responsibility to make the request.

Modifications are not limited to, but can include:

1. Assistance with filling out application forms.
2. Providing qualified readers, note-takers, taped texts, or large-print materials.
3. Opportunity to take a written test orally, or providing extra time for exams.
4. Adjusting work schedules, training, or other programs.
5. Use of a job coach for on-the-job training (contact the Supported Employment-Vocational Rehabilitation Agency).

JOB ACCOMMODATION NETWORK

The Job Accommodation Network (JAN) is an international consulting service that provides information about job accommodations and the employability of people with disabilities, including dyslexics. JAN is a service of The President's Committee on Employment of People with Disabilities. Businesses, rehabilitation professionals, and persons with disabilities can discuss their concerns and information needs with JAN consultants. Information can be provided by phone or mail, and is available at no cost to the caller. For further information on ways to make reasonable accommodations, please contact:

The Job Accommodation Network
West Virginia University
918 Chestnut Ridge Road, Suite 1
P.O. Box 6080
Morgantown, WV 26506-6080
Job Accommodation Information: 1-800-526-7234
American Disabilities Act Information:
1-800-ADA-WORK
Computer Bulletin Board Service: 1-800-DIAL-JAN

STATE REHABILITATION COMMISSION

The Vocational Rehabilitation Division of each state's Rehabilitation Commission helps handicapped individuals, including dyslexics, secure and maintain jobs. The services available are based on each client's individual needs. Services include:

1. Medical, psychological, and vocational evaluation to determine the nature and degree of disability, job skills, and capabilities.

2. Counseling and guidance to help the client plan proper vocational goals and adjust to the working world.
3. Training in trade school, business school, college, university, or rehabilitation center.
4. Selective job placement compatible with person's ability.
5. Follow-up after job placement to ensure success. For a state-by-state listing of Vocational Rehabilitation Commissions, refer to the appendices.

ADULT DYSLEXIC SUPPORT GROUPS

Chapter 10 discusses support groups, how they originate, and what makes them tick. The adult dyslexic can find friendship, support, and empowerment through involvement with a local support group. Furthermore, adult dyslexic support groups give back to the community by focusing on community literacy efforts; participating in special events like Project Heroes; and teaching awareness of the facts about adult dyslexia.

Speaking of Project Heroes, this is a perfect example of program that brings learning-disabled students and their live "hero" together for an in-depth look at how ordinary people succeed in spite of earlier, difficult school experiences. The "hero" is interviewed, perhaps makes a personal visit to the school, and sometimes is videotaped in a group discussion. For more information about Project Heroes, contact:

The Churchill School and Center for Learning Disabilities
22 East 95th Street
New York, NY 10128

ORGANIZATIONS FOR THE ADULT DYSLEXIC

Agencies and nonprofit organizations with services and/or information geared toward the special needs of the adult dyslexic are listed below:

- Higher Education and Adult Training for People with Handicaps (HEATH) Resource Center
- National Network of Learning Disabled Adults
- Independent Living Centers
- State Department of Employment/Job Training Partnership Act
- Project with Industry

- Orton Dyslexia Society
- Learning Disabilities Association
- Vocational Rehabilitation Commission
- Workplace Literacy Partnership Program—U.S. Department of Education, Division of Adult Education and Literacy
- National Association for Adults with Special Learning Needs
- Project EASI—Adaptive Computer Technology

SHOULD I TELL OTHERS THAT I AM DYSLEXIC?

The adult dyslexic can do one of two things: Tell or not tell. Look at it this way. The beauty of adulthood is empowerment. Along with empowerment come choices. You can choose to be silent, or choose to self-disclose.

Either way, you pay a price. Silence means you continue to hide your dyslexia and suffer the consequences. Self-disclosure means you tell others, and risk rejection.

I say, tell it like it is. My expert advisors, all of whom are dyslexic, agree. One advisor, Howard R., is a thirty-something dyslexic who overcame his difficulties with dyslexia and now attends graduate school in Kansas. His story is both poignant and inspiring:

> The positive approach is to be honest, forthright, and have integrity. There are two sides to this approach. For example, in my case at Tom Thumb, a company that supports handicapped employees, they are glad to know…and appreciate honesty and integrity. The other side was a company I worked for years ago. I told them I was dyslexic and they thought I was stupid and a total retard. My supervisor rode me and made my life a living hell. One day his manager caught him harassing me and ordered him to stop. Today, that company is out of business.
>
> I know there is the type that will come and say "I am learning disabled but…" The word "but" weighs about a thousand pounds. There are things they don't want to do because they are lazy and could care less. They want a paycheck, and use their dyslexia as a crutch to get out of doing what is necessary.

Another example is a guy who makes a bad grade on his test, but doesn't tell the instructor he is dyslexic until afterwards. Then he expects the instructor to change his grade and that is not fair. You can't expect the teacher to change a failing grade after the fact.

Most people now say, "Oh, yeah. Dyslexia. That means you can't read." I tell them, I can read. I just want teachers to be helpful when I need help. If you are disclosing, you are being honest with your professors, employers, and fellow workers. Of course, now with the Americans with Disabilities Act, you aren't going to have the kind of problems I had.

When I was a kid in grade school, I was always trying to be like both my parents, who were readers. My brother read; my grandfather read. I could not read, so I would hide comic books inside a textbook and sit there pretending to read so I could be like the rest of them. That was the home thing.

Oh, you know I'd get frustrated because I couldn't take part in normal conversations. Everything I learned, I learned from the television. I'd watch Walter Cronkite, and the University of Iowa had an educational channel where I grew up.

I'd never let anyone know Mom read my books to me. Mrs. L., my English teacher couldn't understand how I was coming up with the answers since she'd heard I didn't read.

I remember teachers talking about it.

Actually, I could have had halfway decent grades had I known then, what I know now. When I was 12, my teacher told me I was so stupid, I would never graduate from grade school. I was speechless and started crying. Living in a small town like that, I had cousins in my class. It was total humiliation.

Then when it was about sophomore year, I realized I had to do something. I was 18 years old, and it hit like a ton of bricks. What was I going to do after high school? I remember to this day, I went to the principal's office, got the college directory, and picked out a school. The teachers made cynical remarks, but I ignored them. I absolutely refused to be a whipping boy any longer. It still hurts when I think about the cruelty in my hometown, but I figure they are the ignorant ones.

Later, in college, I received counseling, and learned through a kind and wonderful Christian counselor that my dyslexia was a gift and was meant to be used as such. My life turned around at that point. And the rest is history.

Someday soon, Howard hopes to teach dyslexic college students. A big part of Howard's self-confidence comes from knowing who he is, and accepting his dyslexia as a gift to be used to help others. Howard is not afraid to tell people about his dyslexia, and it seems that his honesty and openness has its own reward. Nobody calls Howard stupid any more.

Here I want to point out how helping yourself can help your dyslexic child. If you suspect that you may be dyslexic, you can self-identify by comparing your formal educational experience with your child's. Check it out further by joining a support group or arranging to have a professional assessment. Either way, the best recourse is to be honest. By coming to terms with your own "trouble with words," you become an expert and the most qualified person to help your dyslexic child.

BOOKS OF INTEREST

Cooper, Ann McGee. *Time Management for Unmanageable People.* New York: Bantam, 1994.

Unique new how-to guide for creating a personal time-management system. An approach that focuses on the dyslexic's gifts rather than his weaknesses.

Hampshire, Susan. *Susan's Story.* New York: St. Martin's Press, 1983.

An autobiographical approach to the problem of dyslexia and how one person struggled to overcome her disability and become a success.

Hayes, Marnell, L. Ed.D. *You Don't Outgrow It.* Edited by B. L. Kratoville. Novato, CA: Academic Therapy Publications, 1993.

Addresses the difficulties associated with adults' learning disabilities. Discusses how to overcome the pitfalls.

Gerber, Paul J., Ph.D. and Henry B. Reiff, Ph.D., eds. *Learning Disabilities in Adulthood.* Woburn, MA: Butterworth Heinemann, 1993.

Provides in-depth coverage of education, social/emotional, and vocational perspectives. Order from: Butterworth Heinemann, 225 Wildwood Avenue, P.O. Box 4500, Unit B, Woburn, MA 01801, 1-800-366-2665.

Simpson, Eileen. *Reversals.* Boston: Houghton Mifflen Co., 1991.

A personal account of victory over dyslexia. What it is like, from the inside, to live in a literate society and be unable to read and write.

Smith, Sally L. *Succeeding Against the Odds: Strategies and Insights from the Learning Disabled.* Los Angeles: Jeremy P. Tarcher, Inc., 1992.

Discusses the hidden handicaps and is filled with information on adults with learning disabilities.

10 HOW SUPPORT GROUPS CAN HELP

In the movie *Rudy*, the main character, Rudy Ruettiger, defied all odds, attended Notre Dame, played football for the Fighting Irish, and earned a college degree. Rudy did it all through sheer determination. That was then. But what about now? Is today any different?

What's different is the huge number of resources available for the dyslexic child and adult. What's the same are the Rudys of the world, still struggling to put it all together. Unfortunately, they continue to struggle alone, in spite of millions of federal dollars spent to "identify and rehabilitate," in spite of mandated remedial programs, and in spite of community literacy efforts.

So what's the problem? Not only is dyslexia a hidden disability, but the various resources established to help are also hidden. Let me explain why this is so.

Part of the problem is the bureaucratic maze whereby agencies use a round-robin system of simply referring to each other. The other part of the problem is the seeker. Unless the seeker is a professional, he doesn't know the right questions to ask, or even understand how to use the information given.

When you really stop to think, it is hard to believe there

is such a huge gap between those who need services and those who provide them. Federal agencies armed with legislative mandates, as well as private organizations dedicated to dyslexia-related assistance are there for you. In this chapter, I discuss how to maximize the existing system, what questions to ask, and your role when it comes to getting what you want.

One way to avoid disappointment and frustration when contacting an organization is to know in advance what the organization does. To help you sort out who does what, check the index to find the pages (indicated by bold type), services, catalogs, agencies, companies, or organizations are described in this book; then, review the information on these pages. Most of the information provided is free; others require postage and handling fees; some charge for directories.

When making contact, you can request information in general, or make a specific request. Indicate who you are and why you want the information. Some information is geared for professionals; other information is for the general population. Remember, you are collecting this information for your own personal use, so make sure it benefits your purpose. For example, you don't necessarily need guidelines for a grant unless you plan to apply for one. Or, you may not feel comfortable with the response from one group, but love the response of another. That's really what this book is all about. It is a presentation of options.

Another great way to access valuable information is to join forces with a group. The notion of finding strength in numbers holds true when we share a common interest with others. The basic types of groups that can help you with your search for answers are:

1. Support groups
2. National organizations
3. Federal government agencies

I will introduce you to all three groups, giving you a starting point to determine what works best for you.

SUPPORT GROUPS

Support groups are essential for dyslexic children, the parents of dyslexic children, and dyslexic adults. Just exactly what is a support group? A support group is best described as a self-help or personal growth-oriented assembly of like members. How do you determine if a group is right for you and your child? According to Marianne Schneider Corey and Gerald Corey in *Groups: Process and Practice,* it is imperative that "group goals be explicitly stated, understood, and accepted by members."

Dyslexic support groups generally begin with a simple goal, which is the desire to establish a support system for dyslexic children and their parents (or adult dyslexics). The necessity for such a specialized group arises when the existing community system of agencies fails to meet the needs of that specific population.

Dyslexic support groups have one main objective that pertains to the dyslexic, his friends, and family. The object is to help make life for the dyslexic meaningful, enjoyable, and complete. By using resources at hand, sharing talents, and continuing to educate, these groups reap success.

To help you understand the difference between various support groups, I have categorized three basic types:

1. Grass Roots Groups
2. Coalition/Partnerships
3. National Affiliates

The grass roots groups are generally self-help oriented with limited outreach. The coalition/partnership groups are self-help with expanded community outreach. The national affiliates are highly structured self-help groups with a dues-paying membership and a focus on the National Organization's goals, purpose, and agenda.

SUPPORT GROUPS THAT WORK

Basically all support groups begin at the grass roots level, because one person seeks help. After searching for a community resource and failing to find one, that person takes the initiative and forms a small, local, needs-specific, support group. A great example of a highly effective grass roots group is **Marin Puzzle People** located in San Rafael, California.

Marin Puzzle People, Inc. is a nonprofit agency that provides social/recreational services to adults with learning disabilities, and serves as a clearinghouse on learning disabilities. Puzzle People began with an idea and grew to a 150-member, nonprofit corporation, with a small staff and team of volunteers.

Today, Puzzle People offers mini-courses to members on health, safety, employment, driver's education, sexuality, and values. Politically, Puzzle People participates on state and national committees to promote learning disabilities legislation. The *Puzzle People News* is the group's publication that features articles about learning disabilities in adults, news of other learning-disabled adult groups, scheduled classes and workshops, and a book review section.

For information about Marin Puzzle People, Inc. contact:

Marin Puzzle People
17 Buena Vista Avenue
Mill Valley, CA 94941
(415) 383-8763

Generally speaking, coalition/partnerships are structured operations with a paid professional staff, by-laws, and an expanded community outreach. They function on a state or regional level, and have a more diverse constituency than the grass roots groups. An example of a successful coalition/partnership is the Pacer Center, Inc., located in Minneapolis, Minnesota.

The Parent Advocacy Coalition for Educational Rights Center, Inc. (PACER) is a coalition of 17 Minnesota organizations representing many disabilities. As a center of "parents helping parents," it is staffed primarily by parents of children with disabilities or those who have disabilities themselves.

PACER offers training and information about special education laws and procedures and parents' rights and responsibilities. In addition to programs for parents, PACER provides programs for students, in-service training for professionals, and information for the general public.

PACER publishes a news magazine, the *Pacesetter,* by and for parents of children and young people with disabilities; a catalog of publications (single copies free to Minnesota residents with disabilities); and a newsletter, *The Advocate.*

PACER is a regional center for the Technical Assistance to Parent Programs Project and serves parent training and information centers in 14 midwest states. PACER is a great example of cooperative advocacy between groups with a common goal: to enhance the quality of life for children and youth with disabilities.

PACER stays in business through federal grants, corporate and private donations, their Capital Campaign, benefits, and other fund-raising projects. For information about PACER, contact:

PACER Center, Inc.
4826 Chicago Ave. S.
Minneapolis, MN 55417
1-800-53-PACER (in state only)
(612) 827-2966

National affiliations are commonly derived from grass roots efforts that need a more structured strategy to help keep their group intact. Usually, such affiliations operate under the guidelines of a much larger, well-established national organization. SEPTA, an affiliate of the National Parent Teacher Association, is one such example.

The Special Education Parent Teacher Association (SEPTA) is an affiliate organization under the sponsorship of the National Parent Teacher Association. There are approximately 311 SEPTA groups in the United States. The purpose of SEPTA is to bring together parents of children with special needs so they may discuss and address issues pertaining to those subjects. Most SEPTAs are at an individual school campus or alternative learning center.

If you are interested in starting or joining a SEPTA, check with your child's school principal first. If no SEPTA is in operation at your school, then contact the National PTA for the telephone listing of your state PTA office, which can give you guidelines and procedures for meeting state requirements in organizing a local SEPTA.

National Parent Teacher Association
330 N. Wabash Avenue
Suite 2100
Chicago, IL 60611-3690
(312) 670-6782

WHAT MAKES A GOOD DYSLEXIA SUPPORT GROUP?

According to a coalition workshop sponsored by National Dyslexia Referral Center in 1991, participants awarded high-effectiveness ratings to dyslexia support groups that adopt these objectives:

- Create an environment conducive to personal growth and focus on solutions rather than problems.
- Promote a professional and empathetic approach between parent and school, other support groups, and each other.
- Share current knowledge and new information as it becomes available.
- Teach each other and the community how to help children and adults with learning differences.

Other characteristics of a good group include:

Positive attitude	Enthusiasm	Leadership
Well informed	Dedication	Credibility
Offers role models	Supportive, Accessible	Networking

How Do You Find a Group That Meets Your Needs?

Start with your child's school. A group for parents of dyslexic children may already be active on campus. Or the school principal or counselor can refer you to community agencies with existing parent support groups. Adults can check with their state's literacy agency (see pape 170) to locate the nearest adult dyslexic support group. National Organizations with local branches can also help you locate support groups (see pages 129-130).

Questions to Ask:

1. What is the purpose of the support group? Advocacy? Awareness? Self-help? All of these?
2. What is the focus of the support group? Is it disability specific or does it cover a broad spectrum of disabilities
3. Does the group have a charter or guidelines that philosophically match yours?
4. How long has the group been in operation? It is new or does it have a track record?
5. What about membership? Are there membership dues? (Support groups are usually free or low-cost to members.) Volunteer committee requirements? Attendance rules?
6. Who leads the group? Is a professional involved or is it primarily orchestrated by members?

How Do I Start a Support Group?

Hang on to your hat! Don't try to reinvent the wheel. Excellent organizations can help you with the planning and implementation stages for a new support group. There is no charge for these services, and it is well worth making the contact to facilitate your effort.

The Federation for Children with Special Needs is a child-advocacy and information coalition organized to help parents, parent groups, and others who need assistance with special-education issues. The federation provides written materials, training packages, and workshops designed to promote partnerships between parents and professionals.

Current federation projects include the **Parent Training and Information Project** (PTI) and the **Technical Assistance for Parent Programs Project** (TAPP). The PTI Project has statewide parent-training and information centers located in 49 states, the District of Columbia, Puerto Rico, and Palau. The TAPP Project is a national program that supports the statewide parent centers by providing technical assistance in areas such as training, program development, and grant management.

For information about the Parent Training and Information Center(s) in your state, and the TAPP regional center nearest you, contact:

Federation for Children with Special Needs
95 Berkeley Street, Suite 104
Boston, MA 02116
(617) 482-2915
1-800-331-0688 (in MA)

American Self-Help Clearinghouse provides information about model self-help groups or individuals who are attempting to start such new networks in your area. The clearinghouse can help with suggestions, materials, and support. For a free handout called "Ideas for Starting a Self-Help Group," send a stamped, self-addressed envelope to:

American Self-Help Clearinghouse
St. Clares-Riverside Medical Center
Denville, NJ 07834
(201) 625-7101

NATIONAL ORGANIZATIONS

National organizations dedicated to serving the dyslexic child or adult can help build your power base. National organizations hold annual conferences, publish newsletters, review pertinent legislation, support local branches, promote research, and foster professional outreach.

National organizations have a broad target audience as their constituency. They also have larger budgets and more complicated organizational structures. Further, national organizations must readily respond to disability-specific trends or risk losing their following and funding.

Three organizations you need to know about are:

1. The Orton Dyslexia Society

2. The Learning Disabilities Association of America

3. The National Center for Learning Disabilities

Two of the organizations, The Learning Disabilities Association of America and The National Center for Learning Disabilities have changed names in the last few years to more accurately reflect their mission. The Orton Dyslexia Society has undergone changes, too, focusing more on interagency cooperation and teamwork at the local level.

THE ORTON DYSLEXIA SOCIETY

The Orton Dyslexia Society (ODS) is a membership organization whose focus is dyslexia-related research and publications. ODS is named after Samuel Torrey Orton, who was a pioneer in language research, and defined dyslexia as we know it today. Parents, professionals, and others interested in disability-specific programs can obtain a publications lists of books, packets, and reprints helpful in understanding dyslexia.

ODS has 40 local chapters in 25 states, as well as chapters in Canada and Israel, and sponsors an annual national convention. Check to see if your state chapter(s) also has an annual convention. The topics and presenters at these conventions are exceptional and help provide a sound perspective about dyslexia.

The Annals of Dyslexia and the newsletter, *Perspectives,* are two noteworthy publications available through ODS. To learn more about the Orton Dyslexia Society or to request a list of dyslexia-related literature and cassette tapes, contact:

The Orton Dyslexia Society
Chester Building, Suite 382
8600 La Salle Road
Baltimore, MD 21286-2044
1-800-ABC-D123
(301) 296-0232

LEARNING DISABILITIES ASSOCIATION OF AMERICA

The Learning Disabilities Association of America (LDAA) is a nonprofit, membership organization of parents and professionals dedicated to advancing the education and well-being of children and adults with learning disabilities. LDAA has 600 chapters throughout the United States, and an extensive inventory of available publications, with dyslexia among many learning-disability subjects addressed.

LDAA produces a publication called *Newsbriefs* and is affiliated with local and state chapters. The local and state level is where the grass roots effects are vocal and visible, with chapters in all 50 states. For information about LDAA, and how to get involved with a local chapter, contact:

Learning Disabilities Association of America
4156 Library Road
Pittsburg, PA 15234
(412) 341-1515

NATIONAL CENTER FOR LEARNING DISABILITIES

The National Center for Learning Disabilities (NCLD) has a computerized database of learning-disabilities resources especially for families seeking help. The focus of NCLD is to keep people informed, stimulate and advance creative ideas for the learning disabled, and provide both money and technical assistance to promising programs for national audiences.

NCLD has several priorities on which it focuses attention and programs. They are: teacher training; early childhood diagnosis and training; parent education; and transition to postsecondary education in the workplace.

Their World is NCLD's annual publication and is chock full of great information on up-to-date trends, particularly for the dyslexic child who is now a young adult entering college or the workforce. The stories in *Their World* are true-life accounts that demonstrate ways children and adults cope with learning disabilities. One of the publication's features, the "Resourceful Parent's List" includes facts and tips as well as information about recommended books for children and adults, newsletters, and periodicals. For more information about NCLD, contact:

National Center for Learning Disabilities
381 Park Avenue S, Suite 1420
New York, NY 10016
(212) 545-7510

FEDERAL GOVERNMENT AGENCIES

U.S. Department of Education agencies serve as initiators of programs, review existing programs, and sub-contract education/literacy efforts in the private sector through grants and federal subsidies. Funding private-sector projects is a key component, but not a guaranteed one. This explains why some community literacy programs are here today, gone tomorrow. When federal funding ends, so does the program.

The Office of Special Education Programs, the Office of Special Education and Rehabilitation Services, and the Office of Vocational and Adult Education operate under the authority of the U.S. Department of Education. The Office of Special Education Programs is particularly attuned to dyslexia-related issues. When making contact, understand in advance that federal agencies are typically bureaucratic and not always supportive and helpful. Be patient, be specific, and be persistent when dealing with Uncle Sam.

THE OFFICE OF SPECIAL EDUCATION PROGRAMS

As mentioned, one of the jobs of government agencies is to review existing programs to make sure they are in compliance with federal regulations. The Office of Special Education Programs (OSEP) visits each state every three years to hold public hearings about compliance, and to see how schools' special education programs are operating. This review process is an excellent opportunity for parents to provide testimony or written com-

ment about problems or successes, whichever the case may be. To find out when OSEP plans to visit your state, contact:
Office of Special Education
U.S. Department of Education
Switzer Building, Room 3622
330 C Street SW
Washington, DC 20202-2722
(202) 205-5507
FAX: (202) 205-9197

THE OFFICE OF SPECIAL EDUCATION AND REHABILITATION SERVICES

When Michael Vader, former deputy assistant secretary at the Office of Special Education and Rehabilitation Services (OSERS), addressed an audience of parents and professionals in Dallas at a NDRC-sponsored event, he stressed the importance of maintaining a "strong working relationship between OSERS and nonprofit organizations which assist dyslexic children and adults." Secretary Vader said that the main reason such a collaboration didn't occur was due to a "lack of knowledge about key federal laws and educational opportunities."

OSERS initiatives include funding for research projects to help schools integrate children with disabilities and deliver special education in the classroom. OSERS also monitors state rehabilitation programs and provides technical assistance to college and university programs for the disabled. Now with the Americans with Disabilities Act in place, the performance of special education at the grade school and high school levels is especially critical. OSERS' theme for the nineties is based on a trend that shows expectations of society are rising for persons with disabilities. For information about OSERS initiatives in your community, contact:
Office of Special Education and Rehabilitation Services
U.S. Department of Education
Switzer Building, Room 3006
330 C Street SW
Washington, DC 20202-2530
(202) 205-5465

OFFICE OF VOCATIONAL AND ADULT EDUCATION

Responsibility for coordination of all literacy-related programs and policy initiatives in the U.S. Department of Education are assigned to the assistant secretary for the Office of Vocational and Adult Education (OVAE). New programs administered by OVAE include the establishment of State Literacy Resource centers, Workplace Literacy Partnership programs, and the National Institute for Literacy. Lest this get too confusing, if you simply want a copy of the *Bibliography of Resource Materials* or the *Directory of the State Literacy Resource Centers,* contact:

Division of Adult Education and Literacy
DAEL Clearinghouse
400 Maryland Avenue, SW
Washington, DC 20202-7240
(202) 205-8270
FAX: (202) 205-8973

PERSONAL INVOLVEMENT

Since programs depend on the availability of government funding, we can't depend on government alone to provide the necessary assistance. Further, support groups can't function without participation, and organizations can't exist without a constituency. This brings me to the most important point, which is where you fit in the overall scheme.

Never think of yourself as just a parent or insignificant in relation to professionals or institutions. Experts are people just like you. They, too, want the system to work for the dyslexic child or adult, and need your help.

Personal involvement is your primary role and the key to getting what you want from all of these groups. Remember, all groups, all organizations begin with one person who has an idea. If you wait for someone else to do your footwork, waiting is about all you'll do. Get involved and make these organizations and agencies work for you!

The needs of the dyslexic child change as he matures. Not only does the dyslexic have a different learning style, he has secondary psychological issues in dealing with social skills, self-esteem, and coping mechanisms. So, where do you go from here?

Up to this point, I have focused on ways to help the dyslexic child or adult. In the final chapter, ways for the dyslexic to help himself will be discussed. The dyslexic's true abilities and survival skills are both amazing and creative.

BOOKS OF INTEREST

American Self-Help Clearinghouse. *The Self-Help Sourcebook: Finding and Forming Mutual Aid Self-Help Groups.* 4th ed. Compiled and edited by Barbara J. White and Edward J. Madara. Denville, NJ: American Self-Help Clearinghouse, 1992. Order from: American Self-Help Clearinghouse, St. Clares-Riverside Medical Center, 25 Pocono Road, Denville, NJ 07834.

Corey, Marianne Schneider and Corey, Gerald. *Groups: Process and Practice.* 3rd. ed. Monterrey, CA: Brooks/Cole Publishing Company, 1987.

This book outlines the basic issues and key concepts of group process. Included are illustrations of how to work with a variety of groups, with summaries of each stage of a group's development.

Haseltine, Jo Ann, M.S. *Socialization of Learning Disabled Adults.* Mill Valley, CA: Marin Puzzle People, Inc.

Booklet shows how to start a group for the learning disabled in your area. Discusses ways to bring the learning disabled out of social isolation and increase their social and vocational competency. Order from: Marin Puzzle People, Inc., 17 Buena Vista Avenue, Mill Valley, CA 94941.

Family Resource Coalition. *Starting and Operating Support Groups: A Guide to Starting a Parenting Self-Help Group.* Chicago: National Resource Center for Family Support Programs.

Includes suggestions, sample flyers, meeting handouts, resource directory, and a guide on where to find different parenting support resources in your community. Order from: National Resource Center for Family Support Programs, Family Resource Coalition, 200 South Michigan Avenue, Suite 1520, Chicago, IL. 60604.

U.S. Office of Education. *Guide to Office of Education Administered Programs.* Washington, DC: U.S. Department of Education.

A reference guide to federally assisted programs through the U.S. Department of Education. Tells where to apply for funds for programs that serve special-needs individuals or institutions. Order from: U.S. Office of Education, Division of Assistance to the States, Bureau of Education for the Handicapped, 400 Maryland Avenue, SW, Washington, DC 20202.

11 Improving Self-esteem and Survival Skills

Dyslexics are among the most innovative, resourceful, and delightful individuals on the face of the earth. Their struggle with the written word is enough to break your heart, yet they manage to rise above insults, ridicule, and disappointment to face life with humor, grit, and determination.

However, not only do dyslexics have trouble with words, they have trouble with something else that has nothing to do with reading, writing, and spelling. Specifically, I am talking about behavior. Patterns of behavior that directly relate to survival in today's world demand highly developed social skills and a strong sense of self-esteem. More often than not, the dyslexic lacks both. His normal response to social situations frequently leads to trouble of some sort, and he can never figure out why. All he knows is, he goofed, and his self-esteem is shattered once more.

Recently, my grandson Chris and I discussed the dilemma of removing his cap inside a restaurant. He was arguing in favor of wearing the cap and I, of course, was attempting to teach him common courtesy. I used the term social skills to make my point. He looked puzzled and immediately asked me, "What are social skills?"

My school marm's compulsion to reduce my explanation to the lowest common denominator kicked in. I began my appeal with simple logic. Sometimes logic works; sometimes it doesn't, depending on how stubborn Chris is at the moment.

"Chris, the way you respond to situations with others is an example of social skills."

"I still don't get it."

"Check out the men in the restaurant. Are they wearing caps?"

He simply said, "Oh!" and removed his cap.

Part of Chris's difficulty with social skills stems from the fact that he doesn't always read social cues. The other part of his difficulty stems from sequencing and memory problems directly related to dyslexia. This causes him to have trouble finding the right words and to stammer or pause before answering a question.

Language difficulties during adolescence can be disastrous, especially since the gift of gab is central to peer relationships. Sequencing and memory problems can lead to a misinterpretation of events, and a different version of the story with each telling (similar to spelling the word "variation" five different ways in the same document). Last, but not least, is inconsistency in performance. (Remember the *A* one day, a *C* the next?) Because the dyslexic cannot predict his ability to perform, he must constantly adjust to the occasion. Often this leads to feelings of inferiority, and is a major cause of low self-esteem.

There are ways to sidestep these problems, and successful dyslexics know them. The solutions may seem to be roundabout, but they work, and that's what counts. Here are the things resourceful dyslexics learn to cope with, as told to me by the hundreds of dyslexic children and adults I have known over the years.

1. Responsibility

Let me figure out how to solve my problem. It may not be your way, but it works for me.

2. Organization

I have my own system of keeping track of my billfold, my important papers, my money. Please stop moving them to a "better" spot, and I'll get along just fine.

3. Forgetfulness

I do not deliberately forget my chores. A written list does wonders in helping me remember.

4. Resourcefulness
I know you don't like the way I do things. It doesn't make any sense to you, but it makes perfect sense to me.

5. Honesty
I feel so dumb. Sometimes I lie to save face. But I really forgot what you asked me to do. Next time, a gentle reminder will do the trick.

6. Friends
This may not be the friend you would pick for me, but we understand each other, and God knows, I need a friend.

7. Feelings
I have feelings just like you, and it really hurts when you call me stupid.

8. Misreading social cues
Be patient if I goof up. A hint will set me straight; I can figure out the rest.

9. Perfection
I want everything to be perfect, even though it never is. I try to do my best; that's all I can do.

10. Pleasing others
I desperately want your approval. I know I fall short, time and again, but nothing pleases me more than to see you happy as a result of something I have done.

11. Being myself
Please accept me for the person I am. You will never have a more trusting, loyal, and dedicated friend than yours truly.

12. Laziness
My teachers say I am lazy. Good grief! It took me one hour to read two pages of *The Andromeda Strain* and I still have 265 pages to go.

13. Inattention.
Sometimes I have trouble concentrating. It's not that I don't want to pay attention. The smallest noise easily distracts me and causes me to lose focus.

14. Impulsiveness.
It was a good idea at the time.

15. **Inconsistency.**
    I never know for sure how well I do on a test. I memo-
    rized the material last night, and knew it perfectly.
    Sometimes I do okay; other times I bomb out.
16. **Depression.**
    I get down in the dumps over the smallest thing. My self-
    esteem takes such a beating; it's tough to recoup.
17. **Tenacity.**
    I can be very stubborn. It works against me at times. But
    my stubbornness pays off when I set a goal.
18. **Impatience.**
    I want everybody to be patient with me. However, I have
    to really work at returning the favor because of my own
    impulsivity and desire for perfection.
19. **Self-Esteem.**
    Because I make so many mistakes, I feel like a big zero.
    Please don't call me stupid, lazy, or worthless. It only
    makes me feel worse.
20. **Survival.**
    In this high-tech world of computers and opportunity, I'll
    do just fine, thank you.
21. **Recognition.**
    I come packaged in every size and shape imaginable. For
    the most part, I'm just like everyone else; no better, no
    worse. Please accept me as I am…warts and all!

On this final note, remember that dyslexia can be a gift.
Whatever you decide to be in life, you'll come out a winner. Take
my word for it.

Books of Interest

Churchill Forum. *Project Heroes.* A Humanities Curriculum for
Children with Learning Disabilities. New York: The Churchill
School and Center for Learning Disabilities, 1985.

The Churchill School has Project Hero teaching aids, which include pro-
totype kits, videotape chronicles of actual classroom activities, and an
accompanying manual. Order from: The Churchill School and Center, 22
East 95th Street, New York, NY 10128.

Siebert, Al. *Survivor Personality*. Portland: Practical Psychology Press, 1993.

Practical guidelines on how to gain strength from adversity, thrive under pressure, and keep getting better and better.

Smith, Joan, Dr. *You Don't Have to Be Dyslexic*. Sacramento, CA: Learning Time Products, 1991.

Purpose of book is to assist individuals with a different learning style to recognize their unique talent.

Waitley, Denis. *Being the Best*. Nashville: Thomas Nelson Publishing, 1987.

A collection of thoughts and principles that show the difference between superficial success and genuine triumph.

GLOSSARY

ADA. The Americans With Disabilities Act of 1990 (P.L. 101-336). Guarantees equal opportunity for individuals with disabilities in employment, public accommodations, transportation, state and local government services, and telecommunications.

ADHD. Attention Deficit-Hyperactivity Disorder. A neurological disorder characterized by one, two, or all three types of the following behavior: hyperactivity, distractiblity, and/or impulsivity.

ARD Committee. Admission, Review, and Dismissal Committee. The ARD Committee generally consists of school personnel, parent(s), and, if appropriate, the child. This committee decides whether or not to place or discharge a child from special education. It also determines what special education and special services are to be provided.

Assessment. The technique of gaining information about someone else for use in making a decision. It is a systematic procedure for measuring a representative sample of a person's behavior (including abilities).

Clearinghouse. An information and referral resource center.

Dyscalculia. A disability indicated by the inability to do simple math. Arithmetic skills are markedly below the expected level, given the person's schooling and intellectual capacity.

Dysgraphia. A disability in which handwriting is disorganized and illegible (hard to read), given the person's schooling and intellectual capacity.

Dyslexia. A disorder in children and adults who, despite conventional classroom experience, fail to attain the language skills of reading, writing, and spelling commensurate with their intellectual abilities.

Dysnomia. A disability indicated by difficulty or inability to recall the names of people, places, or objects.

IDEA. Individuals With Disabilities Education Act of 1990 (P.L. 101-476), previously called the Education of the Handicapped Act. Parents should note that the term "handicapped" has been replaced with the term "disabilities," and that the act expands the definition of children with disabilities.

IEP. Individualized Educational Plan *or* Individual Education Program. A written statement developed for a child with a disability that outlines annual goals, specific services, interagency responsibilities, initiation and duration of services, criteria and evaluation procedures, and transition services.

Interdisciplinary (approach) or **Multidisciplinary (approach).** Team approach to planning dyslexic child's needs. Services are coordinated by those who work with the child. Team can include: classroom teacher, principal, counselor, parent(s), special education teacher, dyslexia designee, assessment provider, and any other related service professional.

Learning disability (LD). A disorder in understanding or using spoken or written language; individuals have average or above-average intelligence; disorder not due to mental retardation, emotional disturbance, or environmental, economic, or cultural disadvantage.

P.L. 94-142. The Education for All Handicapped Children Act of 1975. Amended by P.L. 98-199 (1983), P.L. 99-457 (1986), P.L. 101-476 (1990), and P.L. 102-119 (1991).

Multisensory learning. Engagement of major senses, visual (sight), auditory (sound), kinesthetic (sensation), and tactile (touch), in the teaching process.

Phonetic (phonics). A method of teaching reading, writing, and spelling that stresses symbol-sound relationships.

Print-handicapped individuals. Persons who are unable to read or use standard print materials because of visual or physical limitations (i.e., physically based reading disability).

Psycho-educational evaluation. Combination of clinical (typical) and educational (maximal) testing used in analysis of school problems.

Reasonable accommodation. Modification or adjustment to ensure that a qualified individual with a disability has rights and privileges in employment equal to those of employees without disabilities.

Related Services. Transportation, developmental and corrective services as may be required to assist a child with a disability to benefit from special education.

Remediation. Retraining of student using special teaching methods that address the individual's learning style.

Reversal. Tendency to reverse position of letters, symbols or words in reading or writing. Example: *b* instead of *d*; *bat* instead of *tab*.

Section 504. Civil rights provision of The Rehabilitation Act of 1973 (P.L. 93-112). Amended by P.L. 98-221 (1983), P.L. 99-506 (1986), P.L. 100-630 (1988), and P.L. 102-569 (1992).

Scotopic sensitivity syndrome. A dysfunctional response to specific wavelengths of light, resulting in reading difficulties, headaches, eye fatigue, and poor depth perception.

Sequential. Builds step by step from basics to mastery.

Special education. Instruction and related services specifically designed to meet the needs of a child with a disability.

Support. Personal support for individuals or supplementary resources for those providing services.

Structured. A consistent use of rules, parameters, and patterns.

Systematic. Methodical, planned, precise.

Transition services. Coordinated set of activities designed to promote movement of dyslexic student from school to postschool employment or postsecondary education.

Transposition. Tendency to change sequence of letters, syllables, or words when reading or writing. Example: *sign* instead of *sing*; *red little engine* instead of *little red engine*.

Tutoring. One teacher or tutor helping *one* student.

Workplace Literacy. Literacy services provided to employees at or in conjunction with the work site and with employer cooperation.

Vision Therapy. Optometric vision therapy is an individualized program directed at treatment of specifically diagnosed vision conditions.

APPENDICES

STATE DEPARTMENT OF EDUCATION OFFICES

ALABAMA
State Department of Education
Gordon Persons Office Building
50 North Ripley Street
Montgomery, Alabama 36130-3901
(205) 242-9700
FAX: (205) 242-9708

ALASKA
Department of Education
801 West 10th Street
Suite 200
Juneau, Alaska 99801-1894
(907) 465-8677
FAX: (907) 465-4156

AMERICAN SAMOA
Department of Education
Pago Pago, Tutuila 96799
011 (684) 633-5237
FAX: (684) 633-4240

ARIZONA
State Department of Education
1535 West Jefferson
Phoenix, Arizona 85007
(602) 542-4361
FAX: (602) 542-5440

ARKANSAS
State Department of Education
Four State Capitol Mall
Room 304 A
Little Rock, Arkansas 72201-1071
(501) 682-4204
FAX: (501) 682-4249

CALIFORNIA
State Department of Education
721 Capitol Mall
Sacramento, California 95814
(916) 657-5485
FAX: (916) 657-4975

COLORADO
State Department of Education
201 East Colfax Avenue
Denver, Colorado 80203-1799
(303) 866-6806
FAX: (303) 866-6938

CONNECTICUT
State Department of Education
165 Capitol Avenue
State Office Building
Hartford, Connecticut 06106-1630
(203) 566-5061
FAX: (203) 566-8964

DELAWARE
State Department of Public Instruction
P.O. Box 1402
Townsend Building, #279
Federal & Lockerman Streets
Dover, Delaware 19903
(302) 739-4601
FAX: (302) 739-4654

**DEPARTMENT OF DEFENSE
DEPENDENTS SCHOOLS (DoDDS)**
Department of Defense
Office of Dependents Schools
4040 North Fairfax Drive
Arlington, Virginia 22203-1635
(703) 696-4462
FAX: (703) 696-8918

DISTRICT OF COLUMBIA
District of Columbia Public Schools
The Presidential Building
415 12th Street, NW
Washington, DC 20004
(202) 724-4222
FAX: (202) 727-1516

FLORIDA
State Department of Education
Capitol Building, Room PL 8
Tallahassee, Florida 32301
(904) 487-1785
FAX: (904) 488-1492

GEORGIA
State Department of Education
2066 Twin Towers East
205 Butler Street
Atlanta, Georgia 30334
(404) 656-2800
FAX: (404) 651-8737

GUAM
Department of Education
P.O. Box DE
Agana, Guam 96910
011 (671) 472-8901
FAX: 011 (671) 472-5003

HAWAII
State Department of Education
1390 Miller Street
Honolulu, Hawaii 96813
(808) 586-3310
FAX: (808) 586-3234

IDAHO
State Department of Education
Len B. Jordan Office Building
650 West State Street
Boise, Idaho 83720
(208) 334-3300
FAX: (208) 334-2228

ILLINOIS
State Department of Education
100 North First Street
Springfield, Illinois 62777
(217) 782-2221
FAX: (217) 782-0679

INDIANA
State Department of Education
Room 229, State House
100 North Capitol Street
Indianapolis, Indiana 46204-2798
(317) 232-6665
FAX: (317) 232-8004

IOWA
State Department of Education
Grimes State Office Building
East 14th & Grand Streets
Des Moines, Iowa 50319-0146
(515) 281-5294
FAX: (515) 242-5988

KANSAS
State Department of Education
120 Southeast Tenth Avenue
Topeka, Kansas 66612-1182
(913) 296-3202
FAX: (913) 296-7933

KENTUCKY
State Department of Education
Capitol Plaza Tower
500 Mero Street
Frankfort, Kentucky 40601
(502) 564-3141
FAX: (502) 564-5680

LOUISIANA
State Department of Education
P.O. Box 94064
626 North 4th Street
Baton Rouge, Louisiana 70804-9064
(504) 342-3602
FAX: (504) 342-7316

MAINE
State Department of Education
State House Station No. 23
Augusta, Maine 04333
(207) 287-5114
FAX: (207) 287-5802

MARYLAND
State Department of Education
200 West Baltimore Street
Baltimore, Maryland 21201
(410) 333-2200
FAX: (410) 333-2226

MASSACHUSETTS
State Department of Education
350 Main Street
Malden, Massachusetts 02148
(617) 388-3300, x118
FAX: (617) 388-3392

MICHIGAN
State Department of Education
P.O. Box 30008
608 West Allegan Street
Lansing, Michigan 48909
(517) 373-3354
FAX: (517) 335-4565

MINNESOTA
State Department of Education
712 Capitol Square Building
550 Cedar Street
St. Paul, Minnesota 55101
(612) 296-2358
FAX: (612) 282-5892

MISSISSIPPI
State Department of Education
P.O. Box 771
550 High Street
Jackson, Mississippi 39205-0771
(601) 359-3513
FAX: (601) 359-3242

MISSOURI
Department of Elementary and
Secondary Education
P.O. Box 480
205 Jefferson Street, 6th Floor
Jefferson City, Missouri 65102
(314) 751-4446
FAX: (314) 751-1179

MONTANA
State Office of Public Instruction
106 State Capitol
Helena, Montana 59620
(406) 444-7362
FAX: (406) 444-2893

NEBRASKA
State Department of Education
301 Centennial Mall, South
P.O. Box 94987
Lincoln, Nebraska 68509
(402) 471-5020
FAX: (402) 471-4433

NEVADA
State Department of Education
Capitol Complex
100 West King Street
Carson City, Nevada 89710
(702) 687-3100
FAX: (702) 687-5660

NEW HAMPSHIRE
State Department of Education
101 Pleasant Street
State Office Park South
Concord, New Hampshire 03301
(603) 271-3144
FAX: (603) 271-1953

NEW JERSEY
State Department of Education
225 East State Street, CN500
Trenton, New Jersey 08625-0500
(609) 292-4450
FAX: (609) 396-2032

NEW MEXICO
State Department of Education
Education Building
300 Don Gaspar
Santa Fe, New Mexico 87501-2786
(505) 827-6516
FAX: (505) 827-6696

NEW YORK
State Education Department
111 Education Building
Washington Avenue
Albany, New York 12234
(518) 474-5844
FAX: (518) 473-4909

NORTH CAROLINA
State Department of Public Instruction
Education Building
301 North Wilmington Street
Raleigh, North Carolina 27601-2825
(919) 715-1299
FAX: (919) 715-1278

NORTH DAKOTA
State Department of Public Instruction
State Capitol, 11th Floor
600 East Boulevard Avenue
Bismarck, North Dakota 58505-0440
(701) 224-2261
FAX: (701) 224-2461

NORTHERN MARIANA ISLANDS
Public School System
Post Office Box 1370 CK
Saipan, MP 96950
011 (670) 322-6451
FAX: 011 (670) 322-4056

OHIO
State Department of Education
65 South Front Street
Columbus, Ohio 43266-0308
(614) 466-3304
FAX: (614) 644-5960

OKLAHOMA
State Department of Education
Hodge Education Building
2500 North Lincoln Boulevard
Oklahoma City, Oklahoma 73105-4599
(405) 521-3301
FAX: (405) 521-6205

OREGON
State Department of Education
225 Capitol Street NE
Salem, Oregon 97310-0203
(503) 378-3573
FAX: (503) 378-4772

PENNSYLVANIA
State Department of Education
333 Market Street
Harrisburg, Pennsylvania 17216-0333
(717) 787-5820
FAX: (717) 787-7222

PUERTO RICO
Department of Education
P.O. Box 190759
San Juan, Puerto Rico 00919-0759
(809) 751-5372
FAX: (809) 250-0275

RHODE ISLAND
State Department of Education
22 Hayes Street
Providence, Rhode Island 02908
(401) 277-2031
FAX: (401) 277-6178

SOUTH CAROLINA
State Department of Education
1429 Senate Street
Columbia, South Carolina 29201
(803) 734-8492
FAX: (803) 734-3389

SOUTH DAKOTA
Department of Education and
Cultural Affairs
700 Governors Drive
Pierre, South Dakota 57501-2291
(605) 773-3134
FAX: (605) 773-6139

TENNESSEE
State Department of Education
Sixth Floor, Gateway Plaza
710 James Robertson Parkway
Nashville, Tennessee 37243-0375
(615) 741-2731
FAX: (615) 741-6236

TEXAS
Texas Education Agency
William B. Travis Building
1701 North Congress Avenue
Austin, Texas 78701-1494
(512) 463-8985
FAX: (512) 463-9008

UTAH
State Office of Education
250 East 500 South
Salt Lake City, Utah 84111
(801) 538-7510
FAX: (801) 538-7521

VERMONT
State Department of Education
120 State Street
Montpelier, Vermont 05620-2501
(802) 828-3135
FAX: (802) 828-3140

VIRGINIA
State Department of Education
P.O. Box 2120, James Monroe Building
Fourteenth and Franklin Streets
Richmond, Virginia 23216-2120
(804) 225-2755
FAX: (804) 786-5389

VIRGIN ISLANDS
Department of Education
44-46 Kongens Gade
Charlotte Amalie, Virgin Islands 00802
(809) 774-2810
FAX: (809) 774-4679

WASHINGTON
State Department of Public Instruction
Old Capitol Building
P.O. Box 47200
Olympia, Washington 98504-7200
(206) 586-6904
FAX: (206) 753-6712

WEST VIRGINIA
Department of Education and the Arts
Building 6, Room 358
1900 Kanawha Boulevard East
Charleston, West Virginia 25305
(304) 558-2681
FAX: (304) 558-0048

WISCONSIN
State Department of Public Instruction
125 South Webster Street
P.O. Box 7841
Madison, Wisconsin 53707
(608) 266-1771
FAX: (608) 267-1052

WYOMING
State Department of Education
2300 Capitol Avenue, 2nd Floor
Hathaway Building
Cheyenne, Wyoming 82002-0050
(307) 777-7675
FAX: (307) 777-6234

STATE PROTECTION AND ADVOCACY AGENCIES FOR THE CLIENT ASSISTANCE PROGRAM

ALABAMA
Division of Rehabilitation and Crippled
Children Services
2129 E. South Boulevard
P.O. Box 11586
Montgomery, Alabama 36111
(205) 281-8780

Alabama Disabilities Advocacy Program
The University of Alabama
P.O. Box 870395
Tuscaloosa, Alabama 35487-0395
(205) 348-4298
(205) 348-9484 TDD
(800) 826-1675

ALASKA
ASIST
2900 Boniface Parkway, #100
Anchorage, Alaska 99504-3195
(907) 333-2211

Advocacy Services of Alaska
615 E. 82nd Avenue, Suite 101
Anchorage, Alaska 99518
(907) 344-1002
(800) 478-1234

AMERICAN SAMOA
Client Assistance Program and
Protection & Advocacy
P.O. Box 3937
Pago Pago, American Samoa 96799
10288-011-
684-633-2441

ARIZONA
Arizona Center for Law in the
Public Interest
3724 N. Third Street, Suite 300
Phoenix, Arizona 85012
(602) 274-6287

ARKANSAS
Advocacy Services, Inc.
Evergreen Place, Suite 101
1100 North University
Little Rock, Arkansas 72207
(501) 324-9215
(800) 482-1174

CALIFORNIA
Client Assistance Program
830 K Street Mall, Room 220
Sacramento, California 95814
(916) 322-5066

Protection & Advocacy, Inc.
101 Howe Avenue, Suite 185N
Sacramento, California 95825
(916) 488-9950
(800) 776-5746
(818) 546-1631
(510) 839-811

COLORADO
The Legal Center
455 Sherman Street, Suite 130
Denver, Colorado 80203
(303) 722-0300

CONNECTICUT
Office of P&A for Handicapped and
Developmentally Disabled Persons
60 Weston Street
Hartford, Connecticut 06120-1551
(203) 297-4300
(203) 566-2102
(800) 842-7303 (statewide)

DELAWARE
Client Assistance Program
United Cerebral Palsy, Inc.
254 Camden-Wyoming Avenue
Camden, Delaware 19934
(302) 698-9336
(800) 640-9336

Disabilities Law Program
144 E. Market Street
Georgetown, Delaware 19947
(302) 856-0038

DISTRICT OF COLUMBIA
Client Assistance Program
Rehabilitation Services Administration
605 G Street, NW
Washington, DC 20001
(202) 727-0977

Information Protection & Advocacy
Center for Handicapped Individuals
4455 Connecticut Ave.. NW, Suite B100
Washington, DC 20008
(202) 966-8081

FLORIDA
Advocacy Center for Persons w/Disabilities
2671 Executive Center, Circle West
Webster Building, Suite 100
Tallahassee, Florida 32301-5024
(904) 488-9071
(800) 342-0823
(800) 346-4127 TDD only

GEORGIA
Division of Rehabilitation Service
2 Peachtree Street, NW, 23rd Floor
Atlanta, Georgia 30303
(404) 657-3009

Georgia Advocacy Office, Inc.
1708 Peachtree Street, NW, Suite 505
Atlanta, Georgia 30309
(404) 885-1234
(800) 282-4538

GUAM
Parent Agencies Network
P.O. Box 23474
GMF, Guam 96921
10288-011
(671) 649-1948

The Advocacy Office
Micronesia Mall, Office A
West Marine Drive
Dededo, Guam 96912
10288-011-
(671) 632-PADD (7233)
(671) 632-PAMI (7264)

HAWAII
Protection & Advocacy Agency
1580 Makaloa Street, Suite 1060
Honolulu, Hawaii 96814
(808) 949-2922

IDAHO
Co-Ad, Inc.
4477 Emerald, Suite B-100
Boise, Idaho 83706
(208) 336-5353

ILLINOIS
Illinois Client Assistance Program
100 N. First Street, 1st Floor
Springfield, Illinois 62702
(217) 782-5374

Protection & Advocacy, Inc.
11 East Adams, Suite 1200
Chicago, Illinois 60603
(312) 341-0022

INDIANA
Indiana Advocacy Services
850 North Meridian, Suite 2-C
Indianapolis, Indiana 46204
(317) 232-1150
(800) 622-4845

IOWA
Client Assistance Program
Division on Persons w/Disabilities
Lucas State Office Building
Des Moines, Iowa 50310
(515) 281-3957

Iowa Protection & Advocacy Service, Inc.
3015 Merle Hay Road, Suite 6
Des Moines, Iowa 50310
(515) 278-2502

KANSAS
Client Assistance Program
Biddle Building, 2nd Floor
2700 West 6th Street
Topeka, Kansas 66606
(913) 296-1491

Kansas Advocacy & Protective Service
2601 Anderson Avenue
Manhattan, Kansas 66502
(913) 776-1541
(800) 432-8276

KENTUCKY
Client Assistance Program
Capitol Plaza Tower
Frankfort, Kentucky 40601
(502) 564-8035
(800) 633-6283

Office for Public Advocacy,
Division for P&A
100 Fair Oaks Lane, 3rd Floor
Frankfort, Kentucky 40601
(502) 564-2967
(800) 372-2988

LOUISIANA
Advocacy Center for the Elderly
and Disabled
210 O'Keefe, Suite 700
New Orleans, Louisiana 70112
(504) 522-2337
(800) 662-7705

MAINE
CARES, Inc.
4-C Winter Street
Augusta, Maine 04330
(207) 622-7055

Maine Advocacy Services
32 Winthrop
P.O. Box 2007
Augusta, Maine 04338
(207) 626-2774
(800) 452-1948

MARYLAND
Client Assistance Program
Maryland State Department of Education
Division of Vocational Rehabilitation
300 West Preston Street, Suite 205
Baltimore, Maryland 21201
(410) 333-7251

Maryland Disability Law Center
2510 St. Paul Street
Baltimore, Maryland 21218
(410) 235-4700
(410) 235-4227
(800) 233-7201

MASSACHUSETTS
MA Office on Disability
Client Assistance Program
One Ashburton Place, Room 303
Boston, Massachusetts 02108
(617) 727-7440

Disability Law Center, Inc.
11 Beacon Street, Suite 925
Boston, Massachusetts 02108
(617) 723-8455

Center for Public Representation
22 Green Street
Northampton, Massachusetts 01060
(413) 584-1644

MICHIGAN
Client Assistance Program
Department of Rehabilitation Services
P.O. Box 30008
Lansing, Michigan 48909
(517) 373-8193

Commission for the Blind
201 North Washington Square
Box 30015
Lansing, Michigan 48909
(517) 373-6425

Michigan P&A Service
106 West Allegan, Suite 210
Lansing, Michigan 48933
(517) 487-1755

MINNESOTA
Minnesota Disability Law Center
430 First Avenue North, Suite 300
Minneapolis, Minnesota 55401-1780
(612) 332-1441

MISSISSIPPI
Client Assistance Program
Easter Seal Society
3226 N. State Street
Jackson, Mississippi 39216
(601) 982-7051

Mississippi P&A System for DD, Inc.
5330 Executive Place, Suite A
Jackson, Mississippi 39206
(601) 981-8207

MISSOURI
Missouri P&A Services
925 S. Country Club Drive, Unit B-1
Jefferson City, Missouri 65109
(314) 893-3333

MONTANA

Montana Advocacy Program
316 N. Park, Room 211
P.O. Box 1680
Helena, Montana 59624
(406) 444-3889
(800) 245-4743

NEBRASKA

Client Assistance Program
Division of Rehabilitation Services
Nebraska Department of Education
301 Centennial Mall South
Lincoln, Nebraska 68509
(402) 471-3656

Nebraska Advocacy Services, Inc.
522 Lincoln Center Building
215 Centennial Mall South
Lincoln, Nebraska 68508
(402) 474-3183

NEVADA

Client Assistance Program
1755 East Plumb Lane, #128
Reno, Nevada 89502
(702) 688-1440
(800)633-9879

Office of Protection & Advocacy, Inc.
Financial Plaza
1135 Terminal Way, Suite 105
Reno, Nevada 89502
(702) 688-1233
(800) 992-5715

NEW HAMPSHIRE

Client Assistance Program
Governor's Commission for the
Handicapped
57 Regional Drive
Concord, New Hampshire 03301-9686
(603) 271-2773

Disabilities Rights Center
P.O. Box 19
18 Low Avenue
Concord, New Hampshire 03302-0019
(602) 228-0432

NEW JERSEY

Client Assistance Program
NJ Department of the Public Advocate
Division of Advocacy for the DD
Hughes Justice Complex, CN 850
Trenton, New Jersey 08625
(609) 292-9742
(800) 792-8600

NJ Department of Public Advocate
Division of Mental Health Advocacy
Hughes Justice Complex, CN 850
Trenton, New Jersey 08625
(609) 292-1750

NEW MEXICO

Protection & Advocacy System, Inc.
1720 Louisiana Boulevard, NE, Suite 204
Albuquerque, New Mexico 87110
(505) 256-3100
(800) 432-4682

NEW YORK

NY Commission on Quality of Care
for the Mentally Disabled
99 Washington Avenue, Suite 1002
Albany, New York 12210
(518) 473-7378
(518) 473-4057

NORTH CAROLINA

Client Assistance Program
North Carolina Division of Vocational
Rehabilitation Services
P.O. Box 26053
Raleigh, North Carolina 27611
(919) 733-3364

Governor's Advocacy Council for
Persons with Disabilities
1318 Dale Street, Suite 100
Raleigh, North Carolina 27605
(919) 733-9250
(800) 821-6922

NORTH DAKOTA

Client Assistance Program
400 East Broadway, Suite 303
Bismarck, North Dakota 58501-4038
(701) 224-4625

The North Dakota
Protection & Advocacy Project
400 E. Broadway, Suite 515
Bismarck, North Dakota 58501
(701) 224-2972
(800) 472-2670
(800) 642-6694 (24-hour line)

NORTH MARIANAS ISLANDS
Karidat
P.O. Box 745
Saipan, CM 96950
(670) 234-6981

OHIO
Client Assistance Program
Governor's Office of Advocacy for
People with Disabilities
30 East Broad Street, Room 1201
Columbus, Ohio 43266-0400
(614) 466-9956

Ohio Legal Rights Service
8 East Long Street, 6th Floor
Columbus, Ohio 43215
(614) 466-7264
(800) 282-9181

OKLAHOMA
Client Assistance Program
Oklahoma Office of Handicapped Concerns
4300 N. Lincoln Boulevard, Suite 200
Oklahoma City, Oklahoma 73105
(405) 521-3756

Oklahoma Disability Law Center, Inc.
4150 South 100th East Avenue
210 Cherokee Building
Tulsa, Oklahoma 74146-3661
(918) 664-5883

OREGON
Oregon Disabilities Commission
1257 Ferry Street, SE
Salem, Oregon 97310
(503) 378-3142

Oregon Advocacy Center
625 Board of Trade Building
310 Southwest 4th Avenue, Suite 625
Portland, Oregon 97204-2309
(503) 243-2081

PENNSYLVANIA
Client Assistance Program (SEPLS)
1650 Arch Street, Suite 2310
Philadelphia, Pennsylvania 19103
(215) 557-7112

Client Assistance Program
Medical Center East
211 N. Whitfield, Suite 215
Pittsburgh, Pennsylvania 15206
(412) 363-7223 (Western PA)

Pennsylvania P&A, Inc.
116 Pine Street
Harrisburg, Pennsylvania 17101
(717) 236-8110
(800) 692-7443

PUERTO RICO
Planning Research and Special Project
Ombudsman for the Disabled
P.O. Box 5163
Hato Rey, Puerto Rico 00919-5163
(809) 766-2388
(809) 766-2333

RHODE ISLAND
Rhode Island P&A System Inc. (RIPAS)
151 Broadway, 3rd Floor
Providence, Rhode Island 02903
(401) 831-3150

SOUTH CAROLINA
Office of the Governor
Division of Ombudsman & Citizen Services
P.O. Box 11369
Columbia, South Carolina 29211
(803) 734-0457

South Carolina P&A System for
the Handicapped, Inc.
3710 Landmark Drive, Suite 208
Columbia, South Carolina 29204
(803) 782-0639
(800) 922-5225

SOUTH DAKOTA
South Dakota Advocacy Services
221 South Central Avenue
Pierre, South Dakota 57501
(605) 224-8294
(800) 658-4782

TENNESSEE
Tennessee Protection & Advocacy, Inc.
P.O. Box 121257
Nashville, Tennessee 37212
(615) 298-1080
(800) 342-1660

TEXAS
Advocacy, Inc.
7800 Shoal Creek Boulevard, Suite 171-E
Austin, Texas 78757
(512) 454-4816
(800) 252-9108

UTAH
Legal Center for People with Disabilities
455 East 400 South, Suite 201
Salt Lake City, Utah 84111
(801) 363-1347
(800) 662-9080

VERMONT
Client Assistance Program
Ladd Hall
103 South Main Street
Waterbury, Vermont 05676
(802) 241-2641
(800) 622-4555

Vermont DD Law Project
12 North Street
Burlington, Vermont 05401
(802) 863-2881

Citizen Advocacy, Inc.
Chase Mill, 1 Mill Street
Burlington, Vermont 05401
(802) 655-0329

Vermont Advocacy Network, Inc.
65 South Main Street
Waterbury, Vermont 05676
(802) 244-7868

VIRGINIA
Department for Rights of
Virginians with Disabilities
James Monroe Building
101 North 14th Street, 17th Floor
Richmond, Virginia 23219
(804) 225-2042
(800) 552-3962

VIRGIN ISLANDS
Virgin Islands Advocacy Agency
7A Whim Street, Suite 2
Frederiksted, Virgin Islands 00840
(809) 772-1200
(809) 776-4303
(809) 772-4641 TDD

WASHINGTON
Client Assistance Program
P.O. Box 22510
Seattle, Washington 98122
(206) 721-4049
(206) 721-4575

Washington Protection & Advocacy System
1401 E. Jefferson, Suite 506
Seattle, Washington 98122
(206) 324-1521

WEST VIRGINIA
West Virginia Advocates, Inc.
1524 Kanawha Boulevard, East
Charleston, West Virginia 25311
(304) 346-0847
(800) 950-5250

WISCONSIN
Governor's Commission for
People with Disabilities
1 West Wilson Street, Room 558
P.O. Box 7852
Madison, Wisconsin 53707-7852
(608) 267-7422
(800) 362-1290

Wisconsin Coalition for Advocacy
16 North Carroll Street, Suite 400
Madison, Wisconsin 53703
(608) 267-0214

WYOMING
Wyoming Protection & Advocacy System
2424 Pioneer Avenue, Suite 101
Cheyenne, Wyoming 82001
(307) 638-7668
(307) 632-3496
(800) 821-3091
(800) 624-7648

NATIVE AMERICAN
DNA People's Legal Services, Inc.
P.O. Box 306
Window Rock, Arizona 86515
(602) 871-4151

REGIONAL LIBRARIES FOR THE BLIND AND PHYSICALLY HANDICAPPED

If the regional library listed below is not near your place of residence, a subregional library may be more accessible. Contact the regional library in your state for a list of nearby subregional libraries.

ALABAMA
Alabama Regional Library for the
Blind and Physically Handicapped
Alabama Public Library Service
6030 Monticello Drive
Montgomery, Alabama 36130
(205) 277-7330
1-800-392-5671

ALASKA
Alaska State Library
Talking Book Center
344 West Third Avenue, Suite 125
Anchorage, Alaska 99501
(907) 272-3033

ARIZONA
Arizona State Braille and Talking
Book Library
1030 North 32nd Street
Phoenix, Arizona 85008
(602) 255-5578
1-800-255-5578

ARKANSAS
Library for the Blind and
Physically Handicapped
One Capitol Mall
Little Rock, Arkansas 72201-1081
(501) 682-1155
1-800-960-9270

CALIFORNIA
Southern:
Braille Institute Library Service
741 North Vermont Avenue
Los Angeles, California 90029
(213) 663-1111, ext. 280
(213) 660-3880
1-800-252-9486

Northern:
Braille and Talking Book Library
California State Library
600 Broadway
Sacramento, California 95818
(916) 322-4090
1-800-952-5666

COLORADO
Colorado Talking Book Library
180 Sheridan Boulevard
Denver, Colorado 80226-8097
(303) 727-9277
1-800-685-2136

CONNECTICUT
Connecticut State Library Library for
the Blind and Physically Handicapped
198 West Street
Rocky Hill, Connecticut 06067
(203) 566-2151
1-800-842-4516

DELAWARE
Delaware Division of Libraries
Library for the Blind and Physically
Handicapped
43 South Dupont Highway
Dover, Delaware 19901
(302) 739-4748
1-800-282-8676

DISTRICT OF COLUMBIA
District of Columbia Regional
Library for the Blind and Physically
Handicapped
901 G Street NW, Room 215
Washington, District of Columbia 20001
(202) 727-2142

FLORIDA
Florida Bureau of Library Services for the
Blind and Physically Handicapped
420 Platt Street
Daytona Beach, Florida 32114-2804
(904) 239-6000
1-800-226-6075

GEORGIA
Georgia Library for the Blind and
Physically Handicapped
1150 Murphy Avenue SW
Atlanta, Georgia 30310
(404) 756-4619
1-800-248-6701

HAWAII
Hawaii State Library
Library for the Blind and
Physically Handicapped
402 Kapahulu Avenue
Honolulu, Hawaii 96815
(808) 732-7767
1-800-559-4098

Guam Public Library for the Blind
and Physically Handicapped
Nieves M. Flores Memorial Library
254 Martyr Street
Agana, Guam 96910
(671) 472-6417
(671) 472-8264

IDAHO
Idaho Regional Library
Library Service for the Blind and
Physically Handicapped
325 West State Street
Boise, Idaho 83702
(208) 334-2117
1-800-233-4931

ILLINOIS
Illinois Regional Library for the
Blind and Physically Handicapped
1055 West Roosevelt Road
Chicago, Illinois 60608
(312) 746-9210
1-800-331-2351

INDIANA
Indiana State Library
Special Services Division
140 North Senate Avenue
Indianapolis, Indiana 46204
(317) 232-3684
1-800-622-4970

IOWA
Library for the Blind and
Physically Handicapped
Iowa Department for the Blind
524 Fourth Street
Des Moines, Iowa 50309
(515) 281-1333
1-800-362-2587

KANSAS
Kansas State Library
Kansas Talking Book Service
ESU Memorial Union
1200 Commercial
Emporia, Kansas 66801
(316) 343-7124
1-800-362-0699

KENTUCKY
Kentucky Library for the Blind and
Physically Handicapped
300 Coffee Tree Road
P.O. Box 818
Frankfort, Kentucky 40602
(502) 875-7000
1-800-372-2968

LOUISIANA
Louisiana State Library
Section for the Blind and Physically
Handicapped
760 North Third Street
Baton Rouge, Louisiana 70802
(504) 342-4944
1-800-543-4702

MAINE
Library Services for the Blind and
Physically Handicapped
Maine State Library
State House Station 64
Augusta, Maine 04333-0064
(207) 287-5650
1-800-452-8793

MARYLAND
Maryland State Library for the Blind
and Physically Handicapped
415 Park Avenue
Baltimore, Maryland 21201-3603
(410) 333-2668
1-800-964-9209

MASSACHUSETTS
Braille and Talking Book Library
Perkins School for the Blind
175 North Beacon Street
Watertown, Massachusetts 02172
(617) 972-7240
1-800-852-3133

MICHIGAN
Library of Michigan
Sevice for the Blind and
Physically Handicapped
Box 30007
Lansing, Michigan 48909
(517) 373-1590
1-800-992-9012

Wayne County Only:
Wayne County Regional Library for
the Blind and Physically Handicapped
33030 Van Born Road
Wayne, Michigan 48184
(313) 274-2600

MINNESOTA
Minnesota Library for the Blind
and Physically Handicapped
Academy for the Blind
Faribault, Minnesota 55021
(507) 332-3279
1-800-722-0550

MISSISSIPPI
Mississippi Library Commission
Talking Book and Braille Services
5455 Executive Place
Jackson, Mississippi 39206
(601) 354-7208
1-800-446-0892

MISSOURI
Wolfner Library for the Blind and
Physically Handicapped
P.O. Box 387
Jefferson, Missouri 65102
(314) 751-8720
1-800-392-2614

MONTANA
Montana State Library
Library for the Blind and
Physically Handicapped
1515 East Sixth Avenue
Helena, Montana 59620
(406) 444-2064
1-800-332-3400

NEBRASKA
Nebraska Library Commission
Talking Book and Braille Service
The Atrium
1200 N Street, Suite 120
Lincoln, Nebraska 68508-2023
(402) 471-4038
1-800-742-7691

NEVADA
Nevada State Library and Archives
Regional Library for the Blind
and Physically Handicapped
Capitol Complex
Carson City, Nevada 89710
(702) 687-5154
1-800-922-9334

NEW HAMPSHIRE
New Hampshire State Library
Division of Library Services
to the Handicapped
117 Pleasant Street
Concord, New Hampshire 03301
(603) 271-3429
1-800-491-4200

NEW JERSEY
New Jersey Library for the
Blind and Handicapped
2300 Stuyvesant Avenue
CN 591
Trenton, New Jersey 08625-0501
(609) 292-6450
1-800-792-8322

NEW MEXICO
New Mexico State Library
Talking Book Library
325 Don Gaspar
Santa Fe, New Mexico 87503
(505) 827-3830
1-800-456-5515

NEW YORK
New York State Library for the Blind
and Visually Handicapped
Cultural Education Center
Empire State Plaza
Albany, New York 12230
(518) 474-5935
1-800-342-3688

New York City and Long Island:
Andrew Heiskell Library for the Blind
and Physically Handicapped
The New York Public Library
40 West 20th Street
New York, New York 10011-4211
(212) 206-5400

NORTH CAROLINA
North Carolina Library for the
Blind and Physically Handicapped
State Library of North Carolina
Department of Cultural Resources
1811 Capital Boulevard
Raleigh, North Carolina 27635
(919) 733-4376
1-800-662-7726

NORTH DAKOTA
North Dakota's eligible readers receive
library service
from the regional library in Pierre, South
Dakota.

OHIO
Southern:
The Public Library of Cincinnati
and Hamilton County
Library for the Blind and
Physically Handicapped
800 Vine Street, Library Square
Cincinnati, Ohio 45202-2071
(513) 369-6074
1-800-582-0335

Northern:
Library for the Blind and
Physically Handicapped
Cleveland Public Library
17121 Lake Shore Boulevard
Cleveland, Ohio 44110-4006
(216) 623-2911
1-800-362-1262

OKLAHOMA
Oklahoma Library for the Blind
and Physically Handicapped
300 NE 18th Street
Oklahoma City, Oklahoma 73105
(405) 521-3514
1-800-523-0288

OREGON
Oregon State Library
Talking Book and Braille Services
State Library Building
Salem, Oregon 97310-0645
(503) 378-3849
(503) 224-0610 (Portland only)
1-800-452-0292 (except in Portland)

PENNSYLVANIA
Eastern:
Library for the Blind and
Physically Handicapped
Free Library of Philadephia
919 Walnut Street
Philadelphia, Pennsylvania 19107
(215) 925-3213
1-800-222-1754

Western:
Library for the Blind and
Physically Handicapped
The Carnegie Library of Pittsburgh
The Leonard C. Staisey Building
4724 Baum Boulevard
Pittsburgh, Pennsylvania 15213-1389
(412) 687-2440
1-800-242-0586

PUERTO RICO
Puerto Rico Regional Library for
the Blind and Physically Handicapped
520 Ponce de Leon Avenue
San Juan, Puerto Rico 00901
(809) 723-2519
1-800-462-8008

RHODE ISLAND
Regional Library for the Blind
and Physically Handicapped
Rhode Island Department of
State Library Services
300 Richmond Street
Providence Rhode Island 02903-4222
(401) 277-2726
1-800-734-5141

SOUTH CAROLINA
South Carolina State Library
Department for the Blind and Physically
Handicapped
301 Gervais Street
P.O. Box 821
Columbia, South Carolina 29202
(803) 737-9970
1-800-922-7818

SOUTH DAKOTA
South Dakota Braille and Talking Book
Library
State Library Building
800 Governors Drive
Pierre, South Dakota 57501-2294
(605) 773-3514 (South Dakota)
(701) 781-2604 (North Dakota)
1-800-592-1841 (South Dakota)
1-800-843-9948 (North Dakota)

TENNESSEE
Tennessee Library for the Blind and
Physically Handicapped
Tennessee State Library and Archives
403 Seventh Avenue North
Nashville, Tennessee 37243-0313
(615) 741-3915
1-800-342-3308

TEXAS
Texas State Library
Talking Book Program
P.O. Box 12927
Austin, Texas 78711
(512) 463-5458
1-800-252-9605

UTAH
Utah Regional Library Division
Program for the Blind and
Physically Handicapped
2150 South 300 West Suite #16
Salt Lake City, Utah 84115
(801) 466-6363
1-800-662-5540 (in Utah)
1-800-453-4293 (in other Western states)

VERMONT
Vermont Department of Libraries
Special Services Unit
RD #4, Box 1870
Montpelier, Vermont 05602
(802) 828-3273
1-800-479-1711

VIRGIN ISLANDS
Virgin Islands Library for the
Visually Handicapped
3012 Golden Rock
Christiansted, St Croix, Virgin Islands 00820
(809) 772-2250

VIRGINIA
Virginia State Library for the
Visually and Physically Handicapped
1901 Roane Street
Richmond, Virginia 23222-4826
(804) 786-8016
1-800-552-7015

WASHINGTON
Washington Talking Book and Braille
Library
821 Lenora Street
Seattle, Washington 98129
(206) 464-6930
1-800-542-0866

WEST VIRGINIA
West Virginia Library Commission
Services for the Blind and Physically
Handicapped
Cultural Center
1900 Kanawha Boulevard East
Charleston, West Virginia 25305
(304) 558-4061
1-800-642-8674

WISCONSIN
Wisconsin Regional Library for the
Blind and Physically Handicapped
813 West Wells Street
Milwaukee, Wisconsin 53233-1436
(414) 286-3045
1-800-242-8822

WYOMING
Wyoming's eligible readers receive library
services from the regional library in Salt
Lake City, Utah.

IN FOREIGN COUNTRIES
U.S. citizens receive library service from:
Network Services Section
National Library Service for the Blind and
Physically Handicapped
Library of Congress
Washington, District of Columbia 20542
(202) 707-9261

VOCATIONAL REHABILITATION OFFICES

Assists and encourages handicapped persons to find suitable employment through training programs

ALABAMA
Rehabilitation and Crippled Children
Department of Education
2129 E. South Boulevard
Montgomery, Alabama 36111
(205) 281-8780

ALASKA
Vocational Rehabilitation
Department of Education
801 W. 10th Street, Suite 200
Juneau, Alaska 99801
(907) 465-2814

ARIZONA
Employment and Rehabilitation Services
Division
Department of Economic Security
1789 W. Washington
Phoenix, Arizona 85007
(602) 542-4910

ARKANSAS
VoTech Education Division
Department of Education
P.O. Box 3781
Little Rock, Arkansas 72203
(501) 682-6709

CALIFORNIA
Department of Rehabilitation
830 K Street Mall, Room 322
Sacramento, California 95814
(916) 445-3971

COLORADO
Rehabilitation Field Services Division
Department of Social Services
1575 Sherman Street
Denver, Colorado 80203
(303) 866-4388

CONNECTICUT
Bureau of Field Services
Department of Human Resources
1049 Asylum Avenue
Hartford, Connecticut 06105
(203) 566-3117

DELAWARE
Vocational Rehabilitation Division
Department of Labor
321 E. 11th Street, 4th Floor
Wilmington, Delaware 19801
(302) 571-2851

FLORIDA
Division of Vocational Rehabilitation
Department of Labor and Employment
Security
1709A Mahan Drive
Tallahassee, Florida 32399
(904) 488-6210

GEORGIA
Division of Rehabilitative Services
Department of Human Resources
2 Peachtree Street, 23rd Floor
Atlanta, Georgia 30303
(404) 657-3000

HAWAII
Vocational Rehabilitation and Services for the
Blind
Department of Human Services
1000 Bishop, Room 605
Honolulu, Hawaii 96813
(808) 586-5366

IDAHO
Vocational Rehabilitation Division
State Board of Education
650 W. State Street
Boise, Idaho 83720
(208) 334-3390

ILLINOIS
Department of Rehabilitative Services
623 E. Adams Street
Springfield, Illinois 62705
(217) 785-0218

INDIANA
Governor's Planning Council for People with
Disabilities
143 W. Market, Suite 404
Indianapolis, Indiana 46204
(317) 232-7773

IOWA
Vocational Rehabilitative Services
Department of Education
510 E. 12th Street
Des Moines, Iowa 50319
(515) 281-6731

KANSAS
Division of Rehabilitative Services
Department of Social and Rehabilitative
Services
300 SW Oakley, 2nd Floor
Topeka, Kansas 66606
(913) 296-3911

KENTUCKY
Department of Vocational Rehabilitation
Capital Plaza Tower, 9th Floor
Frankfort, Kentucky 40601
(502) 564-4566

LOUISIANA
Department of Social Services
P.O. Box 3776
Baton Rouge, Louisiana 70821
(504) 342-0286

MAINE
Bureau of Rehabilitation
Department of Human Services
State House Station #11
Augusta, Maine 04333
(207) 624-5300

MASSACHUSETTS
Rehabilitation Commission
27-43 Wormwood Street
Ft. Point Place
Boston, Massachusetts 02210
(617) 727-2172

MICHIGAN
Rehabilitation Services
Department of Education
P.O. Box 30010
Lansing, Michigan 48909
(517) 373-3391

MINNESOTA
Division of Rehabilitative Services
Department of Jobs and Training
390 N. Robert Street
St. Paul, Minnesota 55101
(612) 296-1822

MISSISSIPPI
Department of Rehabilitative Services
1080 River Oakes Drive, # B-200
Jackson, Mississippi 39205
(601) 936-0200

MISSOURI
Division of Vocational Rehabilitation
Department of Elementary and Secondary
Education
2401 E. McCarty Street
Jefferson City, Missouri 65101
(314) 751-3251

MONTANA
Rehabilitative Services Division
Department of Social and Rehabilitation
Services
111 Sanders Street
Helena, Montana 59601
(406) 444-2590

NEBRASKA
Rehabilitation Services Division
Department of Education
P.O. Box 94987
Lincoln, Nebraska 68509
(402) 471-3645

NEVADA
Rehabilitation Division
Department of Human Resources
505 E. King Street
Carson City, Nevada 89710
(702) 687-4440

NEW HAMPSHIRE
Bureau of Vocational Rehabilitation
Department of Education
78 Regional Drive, Building 2
Concord, New Hampshire 03301
(603) 271-3471

NEW JERSEY
Vocational Rehabilitation Services Division
Department of Labor
John Fitch Plaza, CN398
Trenton, New Jersey 08625
(609) 292-5987

NEW MEXICO
Division of Vocational Rehabilitation
Department of Education
435 St. Michaels Drive, #D
Santa Fe, New Mexico 87503
(505) 827-3500

NEW YORK
Office of Vocational and Educational Services
for Individuals with Disabilities
1 Commerce Place, Room 1606
Albany, New York 12234
(518) 474-2714

Department of Education
Education Building
Albany, New York 12234
(518) 474-5844

NORTH CAROLINA
Vocational Rehabilitation Services Division
Department of Human Resources
805 Ruggles Drive
Raleigh, North Carolina 27603
(919) 733-3364

NORTH DAKOTA
Vocational Rehabilitation
Department of Human Services
400 E. Broadway Avenue, Suite 303
Bismarck, North Dakota 58501
(701) 224-3999

OHIO
Rehabilitation Services Commission
P.O. Box 359001
West Worthington, Ohio 43235
(614) 438-1210

OKLAHOMA
Department of Human Services
P.O. Box 25352
Oklahoma City, Oklahoma 73125
(405) 521-2778

OREGON
Division of Vocational Rehabilitation
Department of Human Resources
2045 Silverton Road, NE
Salem, Oregon 97310
(503) 378-3830

PENNSYLVANIA
Office of Rehabilitation
Department of Labor and Industry
1300 Labor and Industry Building
Harrisburg, Pennsylvania 17120
(717) 787-5244

RHODE ISLAND
Vocational Rehabilitation
Department of Human Services
40 Fountain Street
Providence, Rhode Island 02903
(401) 421-7005

SOUTH CAROLINA
Department of Vocational Rehabilitation
1410 Boston Avenue
P.O. Box 15
West Columbia, South Carolina 29171
(803) 822-4300

SOUTH DAKOTA
Department of Human Services
Hillsview Plaza
500 E. Capitol Avenue
Pierre, South Dakota 57501
(605) 773-5990

TENNESSEE
Division of Rehabilitation Services
Department of Human Services
400 Deaderick Street, 15th Floor
Nashville, Tennessee 37248
(615) 741-2019

TEXAS
Council on Vocational Education
1717 W. 6th Street, # S-360
Austin, Texas 78703
(512) 463-5490

UTAH
Rehabilitation Services Division
Office of Education
250 E. Fifth Street South
Salt Lake City, Utah 84111
(801) 538-7545

VERMONT
Vocational Rehabilitation Division
Department of Social and Rehabilitation
Services
130 S. Main, 2nd Floor
Waterbury, Vermont 05671
(802) 241-2186

VIRGINIA
Department of Rehabilitative Services
4901 Fitzhugh Avenue
Richmond, Virginia 23230
(804) 367-0318

WASHINGTON
Vocational Rehabilitation Section
Department of Labor and Industries
P.O. Box 44320
Olympia, Washington 98504
(206) 956-5055

WEST VIRGINIA
Rehabilitation Services
State Capitol
Charleston, West Virginia 25305
(304) 776-4671

WISCONSIN
Division of Vocational Rehabilitation
Department of Health and Social Services
P.O. Box 7852
Madison, Wisconsin 53707
(608) 266-5466

WYOMING
Vocational Rehabilitation Division
Department of Employment
Herschler Building
Cheyenne, Wyoming 82002
(307) 777-7341

DISTRICT OF COLUMBIA
Rehabilitation Services Administration
Department of Human Services
605 G. Street, NW, Room 1111
Washington, DC 20001
(202) 727-3227

AMERICAN SAMOA
Vocational Rehabilitation
Department of Human Resources
Pago Pago, American Samoa 96799
(684) 633-4485

GUAM
Department of Vocational Rehabilitation
Harmon Industrial Park
122 Harmon Plaza
Harmon, Tamuning, Guam 96911
(671) 646-9468

NORTHERN MARIANA ISLANDS
Vocation Rehabilitation Division
Department of Public Health and
Environmental Services
Saipan, MP 96950
(670) 234-3358

PUERTO RICO
Vocational Rehabilitation
Department of Social Services
P.O. Box 1118
Santurce, Puerto Rico 00910
(809) 725-1792

U.S. VIRGIN ISLANDS
Division of Disabilities and Rehabilitation
Services
Department of Human Services
Barbel Plaza, South
St. Thomas, Virgin Islands 00802
(809) 774-0930

Department of Human Services
Barbel Plaza, South
St. Thomas, Virgin Islands 00802
(809) 774-0930

TEACHER-TRAINING RESOURCES

Educators Publishing Service stocks detailed teacher-training materials and programs for language disorders. Parents may use these materials at home, but should be aware that they are quite complex. The programs include the following:

GILLINGHAM AND STILLMAN

Developed by Anna Gillingham and Bessie W. Stillman, this method focuses on remedial training for children with a specific disability in reading, spelling, and penmanship.
- Phonics technique uses visual, auditory, kinesthetic elements.
- Utilizes phonics drill cards
- Based on syllable concept
- Employs The Dictionary Technique
- Introduces diphthongs

SLINGERLAND

Developed by Beth H. Slingerland, this is an adaptation of the Orton-Gillingham approach using a phonetically structured introduction to reading, writing, and spelling.
Book One—A multisensory approach to language arts for Specific Language Disability Children. A guide for Primary Teachers.
Book Two—Basics in Scope and Sequence of a Multisensory Approach for Specific Language Disability Children.
Book Three—A multisensory approach to language arts for Specific Language Disability Children. A guide for Elementary Teachers.

MULTISENSORY TEACHING APPROACH (MTA)

Developed by Margaret Taylor Smith, this is an ungraded curriculum based on Orton-Gillingham and Alphabetic Phonics. Uses structured teaching methods, multisensory techniques, and guided student discovery.
- The MTA Reading and Spelling Program uses kits for teaching students, in combination with recommended supplementary material and classroom material.
- The MTA Alphabet and Dictionary Skills Program helps students to be able to use alphabetically organized materials more efficiently.
- The MTA Handwriting Program is a multisensory approach to teaching cursive handwriting.

DYSLEXIA TRAINING PROGRAM

Developed by Texas Scottish Rite Hospital. The Dyslexia Training Program introduces reading and writing through a two-year, cumulative series of daily one-hour videotaped lessons and accompanying student's books and teacher's guides. Also offers the **Literacy Program**, which is a one-year, videotaped course designed for high schoolers and adults who read below sixth grade level.

For information and a detailed brochure on the videotapes, contact: Child Development Department, Texas Scottish Rite Hospital, 222 Welborn Street, Dallas, Texas 75219, (214) 599-7800. For Accompanying books and guides call 1-800-225-5750.

ALPHABETIC PHONICS CURRICULUM

Developed by Aylett R. Cox, Alphabetic Phonics is an ungraded multisensory curriculum for teaching phonics and the structure of language.
• Teachers' manuals—outline lesson plans and procedures.
• Student workbooks—series of workbooks based on lesson plans.
• Bench Mark tests—measures students' general knowledge of phonics.

None of the methods described is a quick fix. However, all meet the criteria outlined on pages 70-71 (under "Remedial Methods that Work"). It is also recommended that teachers receive training in the use of the above listed program. For detailed information about these programs and training, write or call:

Educators Publishing Service, Inc.
31 Smith Place
Cambridge, MA 02138-1000
1-800-225-5750

For a list of universities offering specialized courses for teachers of students with dyslexia, contact:

The Orton Dyslexia Society
The International Dyslexia Association
Chester Building, Suite 382
8600 La Salle Road
Baltimore, MD 21286-2044
1-800-ABC-D123
(301) 296-0232

PROJECT APPLE

A model teacher-training program for teachers of dyslexic students is **Project Apple**, developed by the Neuhaus Center in Houston, Texas. The program uses the Orton-Gillingham methodology as the basis for retraining teachers. But it is the community partnership involved in the teacher training that makes the program so remarkable.

Apple (Advocates in the Private Sector for Public Schools' Literacy Education) is basically a collaborative educational effort by the Neuhaus Education Center, the Houston Independent School District (HISD), and the Junior League of Houston, Inc. Here's how it works.

Apple extends 30 hours of training at the Neuhaus Center to one second-grade and one third-grade teacher from each of HISD's 166 elementary schools during the three-year period of the project. These HISD teachers, in turn, teach their colleagues how to identify and work with dyslexics in the classroom.

The role of the Junior League is to coordinate a broad-based coalition of civic organizations and businesses to provide volunteer substitutes for the teachers while they attend training at the center.

The result is a school district not only in compliance with the legislative mandate to provide dyslexia remediation and related services, but also one with significant spelling and reading gains for learning-disabled students based on pretest and posttest scores of the Woodcock Reading Mastery Test and Test of Written Spelling (TWS-2).

For information about **Project Apple** and other related programs, contact:

The W. Oscar Neuhaus Memorial Foundation
4433 Bissonnet
Bellaire, Texas 77401
(713) 664-7676

FAMOUS DYSLEXICS YOUR CHILD SHOULD KNOW ABOUT

Through the centuries, dyslexics have been major contributors to society.
—National Dyslexia Research Foundation

Here is my list of famous dyslexics. Some you will recognize as contemporary celebrities who have publicly disclosed their struggles with dyslexia. Others are individuals from previous eras who have been identified as having some form of dyslexia or learning disability. The list includes artists, writers, scientists, and others who were able to achieve eminence in spite of their "trouble with words."

Agatha Christie
Leonardo da Vinci
Michelangelo
Tom Cruise
Henry Winkler
Harry Anderson
Whoopi Goldberg
Cher
Danny Glover
Lewis Carroll
William Butler Yeats
Woodrow Wilson
Nelson Rockerfeller
General George Patton
Dr. Harvey Cushing

Stephen Cannell
Greg Louganis
Bruce Jenner
Loretta Young
Brook Theiss
Nolan Ryan
Jackie Stewart
Tracey Gold
Robert Rauschenberg
Auguste Rodin
Thomas Alva Edison
Winston Churchill
Hans Christian Anderson
Gustave Flaubert
Henri Poincare

According to the Churchill School and Center for Learning Disabilities the following men also faced some type of academic difficulty, which was most frequently identified as a language disability:

John James Audubon
Charles Darwin
Paul Ehrlich
Albert Einstein
Dwight Eisenhower

William James
John F. Kennedy
Robert Kennedy
Abbott Lawrence Lowell
Saarinen

FREEBIES

The following are available from S. James, Consumer Information Center–4B, P.O. Box 100, Pueblo, CO 81002:

Dealing with the Angry Child
Practical advice to help children learn to direct their anger to constructive ends. 2pp. (1992, N.I.M.H.) 506A.

Learning Disabilities
Explains how to tell the difference between learning problems and disabilities, with a chart that shows language and reasoning skills to watch for at different ages. Describes how families have learned to cope, and what help the government provides. 40pp. (1993, N.I.M.H.) 592A.

Preparing Your Child for College: A Resource Book for Parents
Worksheets and checklists to help you and your child plan for college academically and financially. Gives examples and charts of typical college costs; suggest ways to save and invest; discusses financial assistance, and much more. 49pp. (1992, ED) 510A.

The Americans with Disabilities Act: Questions and Answers
Explains how the civil rights of people with disabilities are protected at work and in public places. 19pp. (1993, DOJ) 577A.

Available from HEATH Resource Center, One Dupont Circle, Suite 800, Washington, DC 20036-1193, 1-800-544-3284:
(Single copies of publications are free.)
   • "Getting Ready for College: Advising High School Students with Learning Disabilities"
   • "How to Choose a College: Guide for the Student with a Disability"
   • "Financial Aid for Students with Disabilities"
   • "Vocational Rehabilitation Services—A Student's Consumer Guide"
   • "Transition Resource Guide"
   • "Education for Employment"

   U. S. Department of Education
   Office of Education Resource Information
   555 New Jersey Avenue, NW
   Room 300
   Washington, DC 20208
   1-800-424-1616
Order: *What Works* and other free publications.

   Division of Adult Education and Literacy Clearinghouse
   400 Maryland Avenue, SW
   Washington, DC 20202-7240
   FAX: (202) 205-8973

Ask to be placed on the clearinghouse mailing list to receive the publication titled *Resource Update*. The collection is sent quarterly to clearinghouse clients. All clearinghouse materials and services are free of charge.

National Center for Learning Disabilities
381 Park Avenue South, Suite 1420
New York, NY 10016
(Free articles and information packets)
  • General Information Packet on Learning Disabilities
  • Information Packet for Adults with Learning Disabilities
  • Attention Deficit (Hyperactivity) Disorder Information Packet
  • "Legal Rights of Children with Learning Disabilities"
  • Information Packet on Learning Disabilities
  • "Dyscalculia," by C. Christina Wright, Ph.D.
  • "Dysgraphia," by Dorothy Stracher
  • "Visual Processing/Perceptual Disorder"

National Clearinghouse for Children and Youth with Disabilities
P.O. Box 1492
Washington, DC 20013-1492
1-800-695-0285
(Single copies of NICHCY materials are free.)
  • "Children with Disabilities: Understanding Sibling Issues"
  • "Parenting a Child with Special Needs: A Guide to Readings and Resources"
  • "Options After High School for Youth with Disabilities"
  • "Transition Services in the IEP"
  • "Questions Often Asked About Special Education Services"
  • "Individualized Education Programs"
  • "A Parent's Guide: Accessing the ERIC Resource Collection"
  • "A Parent's Guide: Accessing Parent's Groups"

LITERACY HOTLINES

Alabama: (800) 392-8086
Arizona: (800) 345-3382
Arkansas: (800) 264-7323
California:(800) 262-2123 (Bay Area)
(310) 940-8511 (Southern CA)
(800) 233-7323 (Sacramento)
(800) 231-0959 (San Diego)
(415) 557-4388 (San Francisco)
Colorado: (800) 367-5555
Connecticut: (800) 345-7323
Delaware: (800) 464-4357
Washington, DC: (202) 727-2431
Florida: (800) 237-5113
Georgia: (800) 433-4288
Hawaii: (800) 342-1577
Illinois: (800) 321-9511
Indiana: (800) 624-7585
Kansas: (800) 432-3919
Kentucky: (800) 228-3382
Louisiana: (800) 227-3424
Maine: (800) 322-5455
Maryland: (800) 358-3010
Massachusetts: (800) 447-8844
Michigan: (800) 537-2836
Minnesota: (800) 222-1990
Mississippi: (800) 325-7323
Missouri: (800) 521-7323
Montana: (800) 338-5078
Nevada: (800) 445-9673

New Jersey: (800) 345-7587
New Mexico: (800) 233-7587
New York: (800) 331-0931
North Carolina: (800) 662-7030
North Dakota: (800) 544-8898
Ohio: (800) 228-7323
Oklahoma: (800) 522-8116
Oregon: (800) 322-8715
Pennsylvania: (215) 875-6600 (Philadelphia
and southeast PA)
(412) 661-7323 (Pittsburgh)
Rhode Island: (800) 443-1771
South Carolina: (800) 277-7323
South Dakota: (800) 423-6665
Tennessee: (800) 323-6986
Texas: (800) 441-7323
Utah: (800) 451-9500
Vermont: (800) 322-4004
Virginia: (800) 237-0178
Washington: (800) 323-2550
West Virginia: (800) 642-2670
Wisconsin:(800) 551-2484 (New Richmond)
(414) 457-1888 (Sheboygan and county)
(414) 286-3117 (Milwaukee and county)

Alaska, Idaho, Iowa, Nebraska, New
Hampshire, and Wyoming do not have
literacy hotlines.

INDEX

Organizations and educational resources in bold